W9-BHG-821

Marketing Your Indexing Services

EDITED BY ANNE LEACH

AMERICAN
SOCIETY OF
INDEXERS

The Authors

Larry Bonura is the manager of Editorial Services at Convex Press. He also teaches indexing seminars to computer companies and professional associations.

Anne Leach has been a freelance indexer for about 15 years and a member of ASI for the same period. She has been president of the Golden Gate and Southern California chapters, a member of the ASI Board for two consecutive three-year terms, chaired the Publicity Committee for three years while also serving on the Board, and was editor of *Key Words* for six years.

Janet Perlman is a freelance indexer, owner of Southwest Indexing. Over the past 25 years she has established her niche indexing scientific and engineering books and periodicals, but does not limit herself to technical books, preferring a more varied diet of projects. She is ASI Publicity Committee chair and a charter member and first president of the Arizona Chapter.

Mary G. Neumann and George O. Neumann have nearly 40 years of combined indexing experience. Their graduate work occurred at Chicago and Northwestern universities, respectively. In addition to Mary's 13 years at Encyclopaedia Britannica, their years of eclectic reading and puzzle-solving prepared them for indexing titles in many fields. **Diane Worden** operates WordenDex Plus, with 25 years of experience in outdoor education, environmental, biomedical, and pharmachemistry topics. A former librarian, abstractor, and database indexer, she prefers back-of-the-book indexing. All three co-authors are members of the Heartland Chapter of ASI, based in Indianapolis.

Matthew Spence lives in Northern California where he specializes in indexes for technical documentation (as well as a spectrum of other subjects for variety).

Jessica Milstead is principal of the JELEM Company, whose consulting business takes her to clients all over the country.

Hazel Blumberg-McKee is based in Tallahassee, Florida, where she indexes legal and other works.

Sylvia Coates is a tennis player, wife, mother of four young men, and indexer—her primary role changing according to whatever deadline she faces. She is a past president of the Golden Gate Chapter.

All selections were reprinted with the permission of the authors.

ISBN 1-57387-054-4

Published by
Information Today, Inc.
143 Old Marlton Pike
Medford, NJ 08055

in association with

The American Society of Indexers, Inc.
PO Box 48267
Seattle, WA 98148-0267

Contents

Preface

The first edition of *Marketing Your Indexing Services* was very well received by the indexing community. It is hoped that this updated and second edition will prove to be as equally useful and popular.

The American Society of Indexers wishes to thank Anne Leach for the wonderful job she has done in assembling these articles for publication. She also updated her two pieces in light of her recent marketing workshops. Her contribution to ASI over the years has been outstanding, and this booklet is yet another example of her seeing a need in the organization and filling it.

Our appreciation also goes to the contributors who agreed to having their original *Key Words* articles republished here: Larry Bonura, Janet Perlman, Diane Worden, Mary Neumann, and George Neumann, Matthew Spence, Jessica Milstead, Hazel Blumberg-McKee, and Sylvia Coates.

From the ITI staff, we acknowledge the assistance of Heide Dengler, John Bryans, and Rhonda Forbes who worked hard to make our deadline.

Enid L. Zafran
Chair, Publications Committee
American Society of Indexers

Many Faces of Publicity

By Larry Bonura

We all know what publicity means relative to your ASI chapter: the dissemination of information or promotional material to further the mission of the chapter in particular or the society in general. There's another side to publicity, though. In this context, it's the quality or the state of being public. It's about individual indexers as ambassadors, or unofficial representatives. Indexers are ambassadors for ASI and themselves. Here are some suggestions on how to portray ourselves as professional, knowledgeable members of the society.

Each of us, by virtue of our ASI membership, *is* an unofficial ASI ambassador. When we bid on proposals, give presentations, talk to publishers, interact with other indexers, we are always showing two faces:

- One is our own professionalism, knowledge, self-confidence, and ability.
- The other is a reflection on ASI, with which we associate ourselves professionally.

Because of this professional dualism, each of us has a responsibility to portray ourselves as professional, knowledgeable members of the society. We need to project a professional demeanor with a solid knowledge about our profession in particular and about business in general.

We need to keep abreast of new developments in indexing and continue to learn how to be better indexers and business people.

Here's a not-too-complete list of some things each of us can do to present the best of our faces to our public:

- Read—Make it a daily habit to read journals and books to continue to learn about our areas of expertise, indexing, business in general, presentation skills, time management, accounting, or other areas in which we need improvement.
- Take classes—Sign up for the USDA classes or take a class at a local college. Take classes in our areas of expertise, too.
- Teach—Do yourself a favor: find a place to teach indexing classes and see how much you'll learn by teaching. You'll be amazed. This can be at a free university, at the college level, or through your company. This is also an excellent way to locate sources of new work.
- Get on the network—Sign up for the AOL or INDEX-L and find out what's going in with your cohorts. It's an excellent way to share discussions with your peers, and it's educational, too.

1

- Study indexing—Read up on the proposed new standards, take a good index-ing book to bed each night and study it. Read articles about indexing. And, of course, read all of *Key Words* and *The Indexer.*
- Write articles—Here's a great way to flesh out some ideas you're working on and share them with other members. Submit these articles to local papers, newsletters about writing and editing, literary publications, and, of course, *Key Words.*
- Attend chapter meetings and annual ASI meetings—Share your experiences, lead a workshop, offer to be of help, volunteer for assignments and posi-tions. Getting involved will make you more knowledgeable and a source of valued information. There's always more to do than people to do it.
- Attend conferences in your field(s) of expertise—Whatever your area of ex-pertise, whether the biological sciences, nuclear physics, technical docu-mentation, or biography, attend those conferences that will expose you to a large number of potential new jobs. Again, offer to present a paper or lead a workshop; it's a great way to get your name out to the masses. Find out about your society and join.
- Become a better business person—Take management classes, learn how to mar-ket yourself, learn about your clients, learn how to track your expenses, learn how to use software to help you manage your indexing business, like spread-sheets to calculate profit/losses, databases to track client history, project management for managing your large projects, and desktop publishing to create promotional materials.

The best way to promote ASI as a professional organization is to be and act pro-fessional at all times. Whenever we as individuals put ourselves in the public eye, we speak not only for ourselves, but for ASI, too.

(Reprinted from Key Words *1/9, Nov/Dec 93.)*

Index Ignorance—A Sorry Fact

By Anne Leach

Lots of literate people don't know or care about good indexing. You can probably confirm this from your own experience. How many times have you played a reluctant role in this scenario?

(Making conversation, showing interest while looking toward the tray of hors d'oeuvres:) "And what do you do for a living?"

(Guardedly, tinged with apology:) "I'm a freelance back-of-the-book indexer."

(Long, mini-epiphanic pause. Then:) "I never realized somebody had to actually write those!"

Or have you ever discussed an index with a publisher and heard, "Can you have it ready by the weekend?" or "Can't you do it for less?" or worse, "We can't afford an index."

Or have you ever asked an editor of a newspaper's book review section why they never review the indexes as well as the books? I have, and was told, "Because we assume every serious book has one."

Or have you ever discussed indexing with a writer and heard, "I'll just get my word processor to do the index."

Uninformed Attitudes

I believe most indexers would agree that we would benefit from an improved public perception of our profession. The writers of books, the producers of books, and the users of books sometimes demonstrate an uninformed or dismissive attitude toward the index. Some publishers believe that anybody can index. This is borne out by the number of publishing houses and companies producing technical manuals that assign indexing to existing production personnel, who are qualified neither by training nor aptitude for the work.

The general public is not sufficiently aware of the value of a good index to non-fiction reading pleasure. If readers don't value a good index, they won't demand it. Book reviewers won't comment on indexes when reviewing books. If neither the book-buying reader nor reviewers demand good indexes, neither will publishers. And if publishers continue to cut budgetary corners, indexers will inevitably lose.

If the industry does not respect indexing, neither will it respect its academic professionals who teach, research, and write on the subject.

Does anybody doubt that we need some PR?

What Is PR?

Let's reiterate what Public Relations, or "PR," is supposed to achieve: creation of favorable public opinion.

3

How does PR work? PR activities presuppose either that the public has an attitude that needs changing, or that it has no attitude, but that either way, the public's attitude can be altered in ways that favor the subject, and that altering attitudes will alter behavior. It's been proven many times that attitudes can be altered through favorable publicity.

Specifically, PR-minded indexers believe that the public's (i.e., readers', writers', and publishers') attitude toward indexing and indexers is frequently uninformed and dismissive; that if they knew better they would insist on better indexes; that if they did so, we would have more and better-paid work. Seems quite simple and straight forward, yes? And a goal worth pursuing?

Hence the existence of ASI's Publicity Committee, consisting of various volunteers who over the years have undertaken to place articles and press releases, promote favorable news, and generally make ASI's name better known in the world of publishing.

ASI into the Breach

What have we been doing in pursuit of this goal? We've been trying to bring the existence of ASI to the attention of the reading/writing/publishing public. We've been offering information on indexing, on ASI, on how to find indexers, on what a good index is, on indexing software. Our mission? To enhance the image of indexing and of indexers. To promote a desire for good indexes on the part of the reading public, writers, and publishers. To make clear how a good index adds to the usability of a publication.

We've been accomplishing a lot on our meager budget, through the volunteer efforts of your fellow members.

Want to Help?

You're welcome to get involved in the campaign. We'll be presenting ideas here that you can use in your area on your own behalf, to spread the awareness of ASI and of the value of professional indexing.

Can you write an article for a writers' or publishers' magazine? Can you write a grant that will get us funding for a public awareness of indexing campaign in the nation's schools and libraries? Can you think up a nifty topic for a panel discussion on indexing at some other society's convention? Can you think of some other good ideas?

Here are a few of the organizations that could be targeted. They're mainly publishers and groups that harbor writers.

AAAS (American Association for the Advancement of Science)
AAP (Association of American Publishers)
AASLH (American Association of State and Local History)
AAUP (Association of American University Presses)
ABWA (Associated Business Writers of America)
ACM-SIGDOC (Association for Computing Machinery-Special Interest Group Systems Documentation)

AMPA (American Medical Publishers' Association)
AMWA (American Medical Writers' Association)
ASIS (American Society for Information Science)
ASIS SIG/CR (ASIS Special Interest Group Classification Research)
Book Builders West (a West Coast publishers group)
Chronicle of Higher Education
Editorial Experts
EFA (Editorial Freelancers Association)
EWA (Education Writers Association)
NFAIS (National Federation of Abstracting and Information Services)
PMA (Publishers Marketing Association)
SLA (Special Libraries Association)
Small Press Magazine
SSP (Society for Scholarly Publishing)
STC (Society for Technical Communications)
TAA (Textbook Authors Association)
WISP (Women in Scholarly Publishing)
WNBA (Women's National Book Association)
Writers Connection
Writers Digest

(It's easy to find more organizations. At your local library, ask the reference librarian to get you their copy of *The Encyclopedia of Associations*.)

In newsletters of many organizations, you'll see an example of the sort of opportunity that could be promising: calls for participation or papers to be submitted for consideration for presentation at their annual meetings. (Any volunteers to design a panel discussion on what makes a good index?)

If you are a member of any of these groups, or know someone who is, and would be interested in finding a way for us to break in with some benign PR for little money, please let the Committee know. Ideal vehicles are articles for the association newsletters, or offers of speakers at local meetings (program chairpersons are always hungry for speakers). It's fun, it's worthwhile for ASI and for the individual who undertakes to promote the idea of good indexing.

ASI at Bookseller's Convention

Here is another idea for your consideration. It's a report of the Book PubWorld convention in New York City in 1991 from the point of view of the ASI members who staffed our booth there. If you live near a city large enough to host such a convention from time to time—or one of librarians, or of the Society for Technical Communication, or of writers' groups, etc.—you might rent space (ASI reimburses these publicity expenses), find a few ASI member-volunteers to help you staff it, and put forth the message about good indexing.

As I wrote these words, the Book PubWorld convention was happening in New York City, and there were publishers and editors and writers wandering past the ASI booth, chatting with our fellow members who'd volunteered to stand there for this communicative purpose and hand out our brochures. Book Pub World '91 will be history by the time you read this, and if I may say so, BIG history for ASI. To my knowledge, this was the first time we'd ever been officially present at such a whopper of a publishing industry event.

Here's How It Was

Not only did perhaps hundreds of conventioneers walk past our booth and see us, but scores of them stopped to talk and ask questions, take home our brochures, and exchange business cards. This was an opportunity to be more visible, and I think we've done pretty well for our first time out.

Let me describe some of it for you. (I'm working from our booth staffers' reports and the descriptive literature sent to exhibitors now, not having had the time or money to go to NY, NY myself, more's the pity.) The booth itself was a ten-by-ten-foot cubicle with curtains on three sides. It had a carpet, a three-by-six table, a few armchairs, and a largish printed sign overhead cleverly proclaiming American Society of Indexers.

Staffing the booth were several ASI volunteers who traveled from far-flung places like Pennsylvania and Connecticut as well as other parts of New York, at the behest of Janet Mazefsky, who as secretary of the New York chapter, put in a lot of hours on this project.

There were lots of conventioneers wandering by our booth, and while many just glanced over and passed on, many stopped to inquire. Of these, many were employees of publishing companies, many were independent editors and production editors, a few were writers. Many knew about the importance of indexes to book quality and sales, as one would expect, but some did not. Many had never heard of ASI. (Sad, but true. But wotthehell, that's why we were there, right? They have heard of us now.) Many were not in positions that required them to hire indexers, but knew somebody who was and that the somebody would love to get their hands on the Register.

So that's the good news: We know that we have a service to offer that is perceived by many as important and useful. Nearly all who did stop to talk wanted to find out how to get a good indexer. Our booth staffers told them of our Register and gave them the order form and brochures that had the postcard order form inside.

Here is the bad news: We have a long way to go to be able to say that we, the ASI organization and indexers in general, have high visibility in this industry. Many publishers have never heard of us, and many derogate the task of indexing.

That's why our—your—ASI Publicity Committee exists. It's a formidable task, and no joshing, to do what needs to be done on limited funds and volunteered hours. And that's why the donated time of people like these dedicated New York Chapter members is so important to all of us. We can be moderately proud and confident that this, our first major convention appearance, went off pretty well. If you would like to join the Publicity Committee, this small group that covers itself with unsung glory, just give the ASI Office a call.

(Adapted from articles in the ASI Newsletter, *issues for Jan/Feb 1991 (page 19), March/April 1991 (page 10), and Sep/Oct 1991 (page 10).)*

Publicity — It's Everybody's Job

By Janet Perlman

The ASI Publicity Committee's new approach, a call for representatives in various disciplines and subject areas, and what every member can do to put indexing, and ASI, "on the map":

Publicity for ASI is a big job! My approach will be a multi-pronged one. Here's a run-down of activities since I've taken over as Publicity Chair:

- I distributed brochures to chapters having fall or early winter conferences and/or meetings.
- I began review of the ASI brochure.
- I'm re-doing the information packets and new member packets that ASI sends out.
- I've been putting together a press list, so that future press releases can be sent out quickly and easily.
- I sent press releases about the H.W. Wilson Award winner to *The New York Times* Book Review, the *New York Review of Books*, and *Publishers Weekly* magazine (they didn't cover the story, but I hope to get them used to receiving our materials).
- I wrote an article called "Does Your Book Need an Index?" for the Arizona Book Publishers Association monthly newsletter.
- I have spoken at an Arizona Book Publishers Association monthly meeting on "How a Good Index Can Sell More Books."

I see publicity as being largely educational! It is common knowledge that the "outside world" often does not know what an indexer does, doesn't know that professional indexers exist, and doesn't know where to find an indexer. Many small publishers and authors don't know we exist, are unaware that somebody besides the author can be asked to "do an index." and of the professional nature of our work. Many large publishers are unaware of the help ASI can provide in finding an indexer through its Indexer Services directory, available free to publishers. As professionals within the publishing field, it is very important that we do a good job of keeping our specialty, indexing, in publishers' and authors' minds, and that we represent our industry well.

As chair of the ASI Publicity Committee, I work on a macro scale to put ASI's name "out there," in the publishing, authors, academic, and professional communities. But there is a "micro" scale, too. Publicity isn't my job alone! To quote our First Lady, "It takes a village."

In a sense, every indexer is on my committee. If publicity for ASI means educating people about what we do and how we do it, then each member can help here. Publicity for ASI means keeping ASI's good name and good works in front of people; all members can help with this aspect, too.

How, you ask? How can *you* help *me*? Simple—become active locally. Join professional organizations in your field of expertise and bring up the subject of indexing in discussion. Volunteer as a speaker for your local group. Write about indexing for their newsletter. Join publishing and/or writers groups locally, and do the same. Offer to make ASI brochures available at your organizations' meetings (get them from me). Help educate people in your community and your fields of interest about indexers and about ASI.

While I'm working on a macro scale, I need all the support I can get on the "micro," or local, level. I hope many ASI members will take up this challenge and help by educating locally, all the while promoting ASI. Of course, if you feel the calling and want to work on the Publicity Committee at the National level, I welcome you, too. I want this committee to be inclusive and representative.

I would also like to have a fairly large group of people from various disciplines and subject areas to work with me as advisors regarding organizations and activities within their areas of interest. The group would be large so we could cover many different disciplines. I need your help—so please do get in touch with me. I don't see this as a big job for any one person. But all of us together can help me mount a great publicity initiative to get ASI's name and materials in front of people.

Get in touch with me for a supply of ASI brochures, to discuss publicity or give me your ideas, to volunteer for the committee either as a "regular member," or as a subject area expert. I am always available by e-mail at jperlman@aol.com, or give me a call at (602) 569-7302.

(Reprinted from Key Words *5/5, Sep/Oct 97, page 1.)*

For Their Own Good:
Selling Publishers on Indexes

By Diane Worden, Mary Neumann, and George Neumann

As oft-ignored and sometimes little-valued principals in the publishing industry, indexers need to be very direct in helping publishers make more money. In striving for lowest production costs, publishers of any size and specialty often risk being penny-wise and pound-foolish. They may choose to exclude indexes from non-fiction books to avoid perceived costly tangibles and intangibles: extra signatures, additional contributors, and time-to-market delays. Alternatively, they may do so because they haven't thought about indexes at all. In excluding indexes for either reason, however, they throw away a competitive sales advantage.

Are indexers as assertive as they might be in using the ammunition at-hand when interacting with potential clients? Probably not, but assertiveness improves with practice and believable information. Successful salespeople believe in their products.

The bottom-line reason for inclusion of indexes comes directly from a book review on the Web, "There is little point to buying a technical book (even one as fun and precociously pert as ...) if it doesn't have a good index." Book industry promotions are big deals to publishers, but a surprising majority of folks who wander into bookshops to browse available titles are nevertheless unaware of or oblivious to them. What really sells a point-of-purchase book?

Consider what people are looking for when they consider a book purchase. Given a choice of similar titles in the same price range, they will buy the one that is clearly written and attractively presented, tells them what they want to know, and helps them find that information most quickly. Observe bookstore browsers: if a glance at the contents page doesn't pick up a likely chapter on what they're looking for, they check for an index at the back. If one's not there, they look for another title.

Ask any book dealer, and you will be told that appearance and content sell most books. Becki Reiss works today for a national used bookstore, Half Price Books, in Corpus Christi, Texas. She prices hardback books 40 hours a week and often receives books that have no dust jackets and no cataloguing information. "If there isn't an index in a book," Becki has written on Index-L, "we are often very hard-pressed to figure out what exactly the subject matter is...and throw [those books] in a pile we fondly call 'useless.' Many of us at the bookstore really rely on indexes to help us sell books to people doing research. You would be amazed at how many books are sold by the index alone."

Is there anything new under the sun? For some 23 years George and Mary Neumann were self-employed book dealers under the name Parnassus on Wheels. They sold used books and scholarly remainders on college campuses throughout the Midwest. Faculty members and library staff would browse and choose titles for personal use or to augment the library's collection. Since these schools had relatively small budgets, books were chosen with care. Tables of contents and indexes were scanned. Lack of an index or a poorly constructed one would usually lead to rejection of the book. Parnassus on Wheels found that a well-constructed index was the deciding factor in determining a book's contents.

Library acquisitions' departments, a specific market niche, look for features that help readers find information fast. Indexes address this point for both individual and institutional buyers. It makes sense, as well as cents, to plan ahead and include an index when laying out major parts of a book. Why do indexers need to sell publishers on this not-so-novel idea?

Popular self-publishing guides are oriented to do-it-yourself entrepreneurs, but commercial publishers often fall victim to their arguments as well. These guides point out accurately that no one knows the content of a book better than the author. The key criterion for index creation, however, is not knowledge of content, but sensitivity to reader needs. Authors have stories to tell, but publishers have books to sell, two very different kettles of fish.

Mary Neumann, with nearly 30 years' experience as a scholarly indexer, once received the following in a letter from an editor, "Many thanks for your interest in doing indexing for the _____ State University Press. We give our authors the option of preparing their own indexes or else passing the task along to professionals. Occasionally we get lucky and they hire someone who knows how to do the job."

Why, oh why, should a university press be satisfied with an index created by someone who obviously does *not* "know how to do the job"? Admittedly part of the problem is that, one way or another, authors usually must pay for the index themselves. They do sometimes manage to get grants to cover their costs, and only then does this lead them to hire a professional. As indexers marketing our services directly to publishers and/or faculty, could we not encourage these potential clients to seek such grants?

Authors develop their own theses and can navigate wherever they want to go within their texts just fine. Readers, on the other hand, particularly readers who are just learning about a topic, cannot be expected to know everything the author knows. They need an objective guide to content that a third party (dare we say, an indexer?), familiar with both the topic and the targeted reader audience, provides with them in mind. Readers, readers who are buyers, must be the publisher's focus.

How much are readers worth in hidden overhead costs? The firm currently operated by George and Mary Neumann, known as indi-indexers (note: intentional lowercase I's), has lost indexing jobs because their estimate was deemed "too high." In one case, the board of an organization producing the work was sure it could find, "a graduate student to do the job much more cheaply." Actually, graduate students are sometimes deemed "free," as an ethics professor proudly related during a cold call. Not a few profs look upon their graduate assistants as cheap labor, expecting them to do whatever scut work they're assigned. Does anyone evaluate their bargain-bought results and judge them even adequate?

Indexers passionate about their profession must consider such potential academic clients, who believe indexes are worth nothing and pay nothing for them, as educational challenges as well as opportunities. Continue to ask, "What are readers worth?" Indexers could provide an evaluation guide before being hired or afterward. Either Carolyn McGovern's article, "How to Evaluate Indexes," *Key Words,* 1(9), 1993 Nov/Dec, pp. 1, 21, or the "Guideline for Publishers & Editors on Index Evaluation," by the ASI Committee on Ethics, Standards, and Specifications (no date), might do.

In contrast to pursuing self-interest, scholarly publishers often prevent indexers from creating a good index by putting barriers in front of them. Unwillingness to consider a reasonable cost for the index is one barrier. At least one university press has primed its authors to expect to pay a price-per-page amount that is woefully low, a fiat that has lost them more than one indexer. Whether indexers who are willing to work for abysmal rates provide good indexes is speculative. However, it is difficult to understand why presses that serve the world of knowledge should undervalue their missions by becoming real-world examples of "penny-wise and pound-foolish."

Another publisher-imposed barrier is unrealistic requirements, e.g., length of index based on the amount of space left without adding extra signatures, without regard for the length and/or difficulty of the book. An indi-indexer client routinely advises them not to index front or back matter, including endnotes. No matter how much one decries the large amount of information often contained in endnotes, clearly this material needs to be indexed. George and Mary are usually able to persuade the editor that the additional cost will not break her budget. They proceed to index endnotes but have cause to wonder why pennies are being pinched in the first place.

Among the hundreds of books indexed by indi-indexers was a book about Robinson Jeffers. The original text was to be slightly revised, pictures added, a new publisher engaged. The author requested a totally new index. George and Mary found a copy of the original edition, discovered topics picked up in one place that were ignored elsewhere, and quickly understood why the author had been so dissatisfied. Their new index was clearly a factor in helping sales of the new edition.

One university press republished earlier works which originally did not have indexes and shrewdly decided to include indexes in the new editions. One of these books was about Henry Wallace; another, a country doctor. Regardless of their subjects' name recognition, this press promoted their books' new indexes to improve sales.

University presses seem paradoxically more reluctant to take on the task of finding professional indexers for their authors. Press management may perceive this as a cost-savings measure, but otherwise the rationale for this decision is unclear. If the press does not have to pay for the index or deduct it from the author's royalties, in-house time and effort, as well as cash, is presumably saved. If the editors do not have to search for a qualified indexer to link up with the author, this too saves both time and effort. If, however, press personnel end up having to edit a bad index, where are the savings? Has the quality movement mantra, "Do it right the first time," and its corollary, "We have no time to do it twice," escaped their notice?

Is dollar payout the real reason scholarly presses forego services of professional indexers? Sometimes the publisher pays the whole amount directly, sometimes the publisher pays half from author royalties and the author pays half out-of-pocket, some-times the author pays all. Because no source of payment is standard and every indexer is free to negotiate variations on innumerable billing methods, payouts fall into a wide range. The answer is elusive.

In practice, it takes money to make money. Especially if an author is totally re-sponsible for payment, publishers' own self-interest would seem to rule, but perhaps this is not obvious. Not only do indexers expect to save money for their clients on bot-tom-line considerations of both efficiency and effectiveness, but indexers expect to help them make money. Why would publishers handicap a resource (their author) by not providing access to a recommended indexer?

In response to someone who asked if a lawyer was really needed for some legal task, Bruce Williams of Talknet AM radio was quoted on Index-L as saying, "Dentists and lawyers are both intelligent, well-educated people. When you have a cavity, would you want a lawyer to fill it? When you get arrested, would you call the dentist?"

Do publishers really *not* understand that good indexes sell books and that bad in-dexes ruin sales? Do presses ever ask themselves whether collaboration with an in-dexer will produce a quality product with better sales potential? As indexers nego-tiating with new clients, shouldn't we take the initiative even if, and especially when, they don't?

Indexes are not often mentioned in U.S.-published book reviews, but reviewers cer-tainly want indexes to peruse. Librarians with library school training who acquire new titles for their collections often limit their choices to books with previously published and favorable reviews. While the fact that a book does or does not have an index is most always evident from the bibliographic heading of review articles, the quality of the index often earns no remarks. This could mean the reviewer has found the index adequate, at the very least. Oblique mention is not particularly flattering either. For ex-ample, a reviewer in the *Indiana Magazine of History* wrote that the "slim index" in a book on Andersonville made it impossible to find the names of Indiana soldiers. In contrast, publications of the Society of Indexers make clear that many reviewers in Britain do mention indexes, and often not favorably!

When *Encyclopaedia Britannica* was planning its "new" 1973 edition, in-house in-dexers were open with their criticism. However, non-indexer management who "knew best" proceeded anyway. An inadequate and confusing index was buried in the "Mi-cropaedia." The reviews were devastating; management's plan did *not* sell the new Bri-tannica. Librarians and teachers could not find the information they had every right to assume should be there. It took two complete revisions of that index to remedy the sit-uation, with the moral of this tale again coming from the quality movement. People who do the job know it best; listen to them. Leave them alone or help them do it. As indexers negotiating for freelance jobs, work on getting publishers to help you help them sell books.

Paula Presley's "day job" as editor at Thomas Jefferson University Press reinforces the impact of indexes on good reviews. "Good reviews," she's said, "result in higher sales. I know that reviewers use the indexes and table of contents when they write their reviews ... I see indexes not only as keys for the reader, but tools for the reviewers."

Reviewers don't want to spend more time than necessary on writing the review, so they rely on the index to find key information on which they can comment. Consequently, indexes are an important part of selling her books to the audience for which they are intended. "Indexes can—and do, believe me!—lead to positive reviews, which in turn increase sales (and raise the stature of the budding scholar!)."

Profitable book production means building sales potential into new titles. Indexes that provide access to content between the covers are not afterthoughts; they are part of good book design and become marketable features of extremely salable books. Indexes are indispensable parts of back matter no publisher, university press or otherwise, can afford to ignore.

Of course, during our marketing interactions, every indexer cannot forget that he or she is promoting a very specialized service. By default, each of us represents all other indexers. This is neither magnanimous nor impractical; it is level-headed business acumen on the one hand and the way the cookie crumbles on the other. As business people, we help clients and those whom we'd like to be our clients solve problems they face.

Publishers, who may be initially reluctant to engage an indexer making a cold call, may not know how to find qualified indexers. Our job is to help them find a knowledgeable indexer who works within recommended standards for the subject they need to sell. Yes, tell them about the ASI Website at http://www.well.com/user/asi, send them a Special Interest Group directory if appropriate, or direct them to e-mail asi@well.com for other referrals from "Indexer Services." Give them ASI's voicemail number, 206-241-9196, to help find someone with experience, perhaps within their own geographical area. Of course, you too may be available.

When publishers obtain professional indexers, they have first-hand help with a variety of problems, including provision of an objective guide to the text. Indexers also catch variations in titles of publications, organizations, personal names, etc., which copy editors may miss because many pages may separate their mentions. The intervening pages serve to conceal them. A good indexer will query the editor and track down the correct version to improve the book's accuracy, an auxiliary service most editors appreciate.

To sell publishers on indexes, believe in yourself and others in your profession. Reiterate three major points and mention the minor points when given half a chance during cold calls or the negotiating process:

- Indexes sell new books and resell used books. They add competitive value by generating good reviews. Indexes appeal to browser, library, academic, and research markets.
- Trained indexers are partners with authors and publishers. They expect to save clients money and expect to help them make money. Because sales cancel costs, indexes cost little or nothing, but initially are not free. Everyone gets what they pay for.
- Cash is a four-letter word that can mean quality. Readers and publishers buy quality that indexes provide. Evaluation tools do exist.

Indexing doesn't sell itself, but indexes do when indexers approach publishers with positive, bottom-line proposals. Making a living, even real money, is a goal both share. Indexes created by professional indexers add quality, a value none of us can afford to lose.

(Reprinted from Key Words *5/5, Sep/Oct 97, page 4.)*

How to Get Clients

By Matthew Spence

As someone observed at an ASI meeting I attended not long ago, the very preferences and qualities that make us good indexers—bookishness, working well alone, a tolerance for long periods of concentrated work, an interest in conversations with individuals present only in print—are the same qualities that make it difficult for many of us to build our indexing as a business. As a result, ASI loses some 30 percent of new members after one year, at least in part because many aspiring freelancers are unable to turn an interest in indexing into a livelihood.

From my own experience building an indexing business in the last year and a half, I know that there are many factors that contribute to a successful start in freelance indexing. For me, it started with an intuition that indexing was like a gift fallen from the sky at a moment in my life when I needed to make a fresh start in how I made a living. Beyond my own efforts, I am forever indebted to the magnanimity of indexing colleagues and friends who encouraged and helped me to get started, as well as to tremendous good fortune at various critical points in the process.

One of the secrets of starting a business, however, is taking all that potential and support and actually doing something with it. In this regard, an essential ingredient in getting started was a systematic approach to marketing my services as an indexer. I knew I needed a plan that would ensure that, whether I felt like it or not, I made contact with individuals who, over time, would give me the jobs that would pay the bills and keep me in business.

Listed here are a loosely organized series of observations, ideas, strategies, principles, and plain old kick-yourself-in-the-pants requirements that, taken all together, helped put me in business as a freelance indexer in less than a year. I have also noted throughout some of the other factors that have contributed to making my particular approach to freelancing both successful and enjoyable.

Overcoming Your Own Resistance

Marketing your services as an indexer is not difficult and can be a lot of fun. But, if you are anything like me, you may have to break through a level of (sometimes) nasty resistance to do it.

Let me begin by saying that until I had to sell my services as an indexer, I *dreaded* sales. When I left college 20 years ago and suddenly realized that business is an essential component of adult life and all business is essentially about sales, my heart sank. I just wasn't that kind of guy—or at least I didn't think I was. When it came to marketing my indexing services, after 20 years in various jobs and careers, I finally found that I had enough emotional stamina or whatever to actually get on the phone and sell. Because I liked the product and had confidence in the service, I found I actually enjoyed the selling. Now, I think I am bullish on marketing as essential to success as an indexer because through indexing I have discovered, and now finally understand, the fun of starting a business and doing the selling that builds it.

That being said, here are a few things I have observed about the market for indexing services. Basically, editors and production managers are looking for good indexers. Although they may not need you right now, they know there will come a time when they will need an indexer and their regular indexers are not available. So, in my experience, editors and production managers are usually interested in knowing about you and your services, they do keep résumés on file, and they do call back when they have a need, even a year or more after your first contact.

You may find, however, that the marketing method I describe may be more effective with some prospects than with others. My own experience comes primarily from marketing to software manufacturers and publishers of computer books. These are both high-volume, fast-paced industries, whose documentation and editorial departments are driven by aggressive marketing plans and very demanding deadlines. There is usually a steady turnover in personnel. Therefore, in most cases the editors and production managers I talk to have no problem hiring someone who is relatively new to the field and looking to break in on the action.

Trade and academic publishers, however, may be of a somewhat different disposition. The volume of work they handle is often smaller (speaking mostly about West Coast publishers here) and the pace of the industry is somewhat slower than computer publishers. So, they may be more reserved when approached by someone selling services, and it may take longer before they have a need for a new indexer because they are loyal to their regular freelancers, some of whom are former colleagues.

In general, marketing is a game of numbers and time. If you make the contacts and send résumés, in time those contacts will give you work. The key, however, is to make your contacts personal and to gently, but persistently, cultivate the relationships you make.

Make Marketing Your Job

When you are not working on an index, your *job* is to get work.

One of the most difficult things I found about starting a new business was that when I wasn't working on a project I felt unemployed. And few things I have experienced are more demoralizing than feeling unemployed.

So, when you are not working on an index, make marketing your job. Do it eight hours a day (or at least six), as a discipline. Make a plan and stick to it. Don't let yourself off the hook, unless your disposition is affecting your ability to be forthright and personable. If you absolutely can't make calls today, do research, make a plan for tomorrow, write a phone script, work on your résumé, anything, but keep working at your new job: selling your services.

I suggest you make your calls in the morning and write your follow-up letters in the afternoon. It will get you work. And it helps to cut into the depressing illusion that you are "unemployed."

Locating Your Market

The creative part of marketing is identifying a portion of the market you are interested in and have qualifications for—ideally one that others might not as readily think of approaching. Then, you must figure out how to locate your market and how to sell your services to it.

To locate prospects in publishing, a good source is the *Writer's Market*, a guide to publishers updated annually, available in any Waldenbooks, B. Dalton, or other bookstores. Indexers also consult the *Literary Marketplace* (*LMP*) at their local libraries for names of publishers. The Writer's Connection, 1601 Saratoga-Sunnyvale Road, Suite 180, Cupertino, CA 95014, (408) 973-0227 publishes directories for publishers in California and Hawaii, the Northwest, and the Southwest. There may be sources for regional directories in other parts of the country. For corporate prospects, try *Dun & Bradstreet's Million Dollar Directory* (also in most libraries).

Tell everyone you know about your new business. Explain it to them, get their interest. You never know what ideas or contacts friends and casual contacts may have for you to pursue.

Preparing Your Tools and Materials

Before you start calling, be prepared to do your follow-up by mail. I do all my correspondence on a laser printer in an attractive typeface (something other than Courier). Before I could afford a laser printer, I used a friend's and kept all my correspondence files on a floppy disk. I discovered recently that I can even print mailing labels, business cards, and Rolodex cards on my laser printer.

If you cannot afford and do not have access to a laser printer, have stationery printed, along with a business or Rolodex card. Nothing fancy is required—just clean, simple, and professional: name, "Indexing Services," address, and phone number.

Similarly, take the time to compose and lay out your résumé simply and attractively on a single page. Start by including all information and experience that might be relevant and then edit and condense until it fits on one page. Print it or have it printed on a laser printer. Consult books on résumés at your library for style. I found *A Damn Good Résumé*, by Yana Parker (Ten Speed Press) to be very helpful.

A "damn good résumé" (or at least a good one) is definitely a plus when marketing your services. You need to establish your credentials. And whereas many of us over the years have become cynical about résumés and their effectiveness, I was surprised to find that prospects would actually say, "Yes, I got your letter—good résumé."

I had my own particular qualifications for the market I was going after: an Ivy League education and experience both with computers and in publishing. You will have to find your own. There is a process of self-discovery required to put together a good résumé. And you may need the help of a friend or intimate who knows you well and loves you, who can help you see strengths you tend to overlook, and who will help you promote your capabilities without feeling like you're being conceited or just downright sinful.

The trick, or the art, is to find, among all the things you know and have done and like to do and are good at, a unique combination of qualities and qualifications that makes your résumé different, even just a little bit, so it is notable. Think creatively. Let it cook for a while. And never stop fine tuning it. I invariably make some change in mine every time I happen to look at it.

OK, enough busy work. Now for the real stuff.

The "Call-Send-Call" Formula

The classic formula for telephone sales is called "Call-Send-Call."

CALL first and make contact with the individual responsible for hiring.

Then, SEND a follow-up letter with a résumé and a business card, references, and a sample index if requested.

Finally, CALL BACK in one to two weeks to see that your contact has received the materials and reviewed them and to initiate the next step: do they have a job for you?

Making Those Calls

When cold calling publishers, there is no need, in my experience, to be strategic about "getting in the door."

When I first started calling publishers, I would say as authoritatively as I could, "The managing editor, please." Understandably, I usually ended up in some runaround with the receptionist.

I finally learned that all I needed was to tell the receptionist what I wanted and she was usually more than happy to help, even if she didn't know what I was talking about.

"I am a freelance indexer. I am calling to find out if XYZ Company uses freelance indexers and who in your organization I would talk to about that."

When talking to the person responsible (usually the managing editor or the production manager), ask them if XYZ Company uses freelance indexers and how you go about becoming one of the indexers they use. The conversation should proceed very naturally from there.

What About Previous Indexing Experience?

Probably the biggest hurdle in getting started in indexing is the Catch-22 that, in general, you have to have done work to get work.

A prospect will invariably ask you what you have indexed or who you have worked for. Some will ask for a sample of your work. So, when cold calling, you need to have done enough indexing to be able to talk shop. You need to be able to talk about how you approach a project, tell some war stories (even if you have only done a few books), tell what you will need from them, talk about their style and how they will want the index delivered. You need to be able to establish your professional credibility by carrying your end in a professional conversation about indexing.

Your contact will probably figure out that you are new, if only because you are calling and they've never heard of you before (publishing is a small world). That's fine, everyone has to begin somewhere. But there is a difference between being new and being inexperienced.

Apart from the prospect's interest in your experience, you also need to have done enough indexing to be confident about your capabilities as an indexer. Half your ability to market yourself as an indexer comes from your confidence in yourself and your work, and that comes from experience.

There are a number of ways to deal with the need for experience.

Professional training as an indexer is essential preparation for a freelance indexer and can go some distance toward establishing your credibility as someone new to the field. So can knowledge of or experience in the field you are looking to index for. If you have taken an indexing course, you have written indexes that may be able to serve as samples.

Indexers who have taken the U.S. Department of Agriculture Applied Indexing correspondence course (in which you write and get feedback on 10 indexes) tell me that it gives invaluable experience in indexing that goes a long way toward building self-confidence. (Contact the Correspondence Study Program, Graduate School USDA, South Agriculture Bldg., Rm. 1114, 14th & Independence Ave. SW, Washington, D.C. 20250, (202) 720-7123, for course descriptions and registration information.)

Some indexers have started by doing volunteer work for organizations or friends who are publishing books or journals. Many of us have interests in non-profit organizations that may be able to use our volunteer services as indexers.

An invaluable resource for fledgling indexers is, of course, other indexers. In a pinch, an indexer you know may ask you to pick up a job they cannot handle because of schedule conflicts, refer an inquiry to you, or give you ideas for prospects to pursue.

Established indexers are a wealth of inspiration, encouragement, and practical advice on getting started as a freelancer. Contact with other indexers through participation in the local ASI chapter is for many the essential ingredient to becoming established in a career in indexing. But ASI is not just a clearinghouse for jobs. It is the professional organization dedicated to advancing the art and science of indexing. It will serve your professional training and also ask for your participation. Those who are established continue to participate in ASI as a way to repay the "debt" to the organization that helped them get their start.

On this particular score, I was incredibly fortunate. Through friends who are indexers, I learned of an indexer who was willing to start me without previous experience (although I had taken a 10-week indexing course at the U.C. Berkeley Extension). Having done five or six indexes, I was ready to go directly to publishers myself.

The Follow-Up Letter

After you have made a contact with someone who is interested in your indexing services (or even just open to receiving your résumé), send your follow-up letter as soon as you can, while the conversation is fresh in the prospect's mind.

Send a one-page cover letter thanking the individual for the time taken to speak with you (or whatever lead-in feels right). Then briefly summarize the strong or most relevant points of your résumé and answer any questions that were asked about rates, delivery methods, your expertise, etc. In your closing state when you will contact the company next. Enclose your résumé and business card. Type (rather than handwrite) the envelope.

The body of your cover letter can be a boilerplate you set up on your word processor. Just change the name and address, personalize the opening and closing paragraphs, and add or delete the paragraphs describing your services according to what was discussed in the initial contact.

I've included a generic sample of the cover letter and résumé I use (loosely tailored to my specialization in computer documentation):

Matthew Spence Indexing Services
PO Box 1234
Any City, USA

October 26, 1992

Ms. Edi Tor
U-NameIt Software Company
I/O Address
Silicon Valley, CA 95555

Dear Edi,

Thank you for the time you took with me yesterday to discuss your indexing needs at U-NameIt Software.

As you suggested, I am sending my résumé, a sample of my technical indexing, and a list of current references.

As you will see from my résumé, a Harvard education in the liberal arts and broad professional experience prepare me well as an indexer in a wide range of subjects in both general and technical fields.

In addition to my competence as a professional indexer, I have 10 years' experience with computers. I was trained in the use of business applications software for databases, spreadsheets, graphics, economic simulation, project management, etc., 10 years ago when such things were only available on mainframes. I sold and supported time-sharing services to clients in the oil industry and taught seminars to our clients. Since 1986, I have used PCs and Macintosh computers extensively in a range of capacities necessary to operate and manage a small publishing company.

As a result of this background, I am thoroughly computer literate and have a solid end user's appreciation for technical manuals and the essential role of indexes in them.

I can deliver completed indexes on disk and hard copy by Federal Express, or by modem transmission, in a number of different file formats for both PCs and Macintosh computers. I am accustomed to working under demanding deadlines.

I look forward to working with you on a project. I will call you in the coming week to discuss how we proceed from here.

Regards,

Matthew Spence

Matthew Spence Indexing Services
PO Box 1234
Any City, USA

OBJECTIVE: Employment as a trade, technical, and academic indexer

QUALIFICATIONS
- thoughtfully constructed indexes tailored to your specifications
- qualified in general, academic, and technical subject areas
- punctual delivery by courier or modem
- will work under demanding deadlines
- member, American Society of Indexers

RECENT CLIENTS include:
- Technobabble Computer Books
- Oranges and Apples Computer Company
- Idiot's Delight Software
- Podunk University Press

AREAS OF COMPETENCE
Ten years' experience with mainframes, PCs, and Macintosh computers provides
strong competence for:
- computer publications and technical documentation

Indexing experience, a Harvard education, a sub-career as a teacher, and a
passion for books also provide strong background in:
- General Science
- Social Sciences
- Political Science
- Health
- Psychology
- Humanities

EMPLOYMENT HISTORY
1991–present | Freelance indexer

Writer and Editor
1982–1990 | The Dawn Horse Press, Clearlake, CA
Spence & Co., Stockbridge MA

Teacher:
1984–1990 | Secondary schools in New York, California, and Fiji
Adult education courses

Economic Analyst:
1982 | Litigation Support Group, San Rafael CA

Software sales and support:
1981 | The Service Bureau Company, Houston TX

Management and Business:
1976–81 | Management positions in banking, import/export

EDUCATION
University of California Extension, Berkeley
Professionally trained as an indexer by Nancy Mulvany, Bayside Indexing,
past-president, American Society of Indexers
Harvard University, Cambridge MA, B.A. cum laude in Social Studies, 1973

The Call-Back

One to two weeks after you send the follow-up letter, call again to confirm that the material was received and reviewed and to ask what the next step is. Do they have a job for you? When do they expect to? When should you call again?

I have never had anyone just brush me off, either on a cold call or a follow-up call. Even on cold calls when the prospect does not understand at first what I do (this happens, especially with corporate prospects), a simple explanation usually leads to a fruitful conversation about their needs and my services. An open and forthright manner is accepted as professional. Sales is not a dirty word.

Ask for More Work from Satisfied Clients

Unlike other things in life, work *does not* happen: you have to ask for it. I find this to be true even with my best clients.

A client who likes your work is generally happy to keep you busy and in business. But whereas you have only one thing on your mind (more indexes), editors or production managers have so many details to handle in the final stages of book production that they are frequently not thinking about the index the way you are. So they often appreciate a call from you offering to handle one of those details—the index.

If you haven't heard from a publisher you have written a good index for, don't be bashful. Call them up and ask for more.

Having Money to Live On

Finally, to make money, you have to expend time and energy, as I have indicated. But to make money, you also have to spend money. An essential part of marketing a new business is making sure you have enough money or other means to live on while you are working to get the business going.

A pamphlet I picked up from the Small Business Administration early in my start as an indexer gave important advice about starting a business:

First, expect to spend from 60 to 70 hours a week on the business for the first year. Starting an indexing business may not require quite this much, but getting started is a full-time enterprise, even before you get your first job.

Second, if you need to borrow money to start a business, get as much money as you possibly can, whether from a bank or from friends and relatives. If you don't want to borrow, be sure your savings can keep you going for several months. In other words, be sure you are properly capitalized.

While getting your first jobs will be exhilarating, they may not be enough to support you. But after all you have invested in time and equipment, you cannot afford to have to take other work and not be able to accept indexing jobs when they come in. You need to be at home, on the phone (get Call Waiting), or at least by the phone (getting your nerve up for the next call), available to accept a job when a prospect finally calls you back.

You have to be able to survive the early months when business is slow and your primary job is letting people know you are available. In addition to living costs and your initial investment in equipment, you should plan to spend several hundred dollars on phone calls and supplies in your first few months, depending, of course, on how aggressively you market. Bottom line, you need enough money to do whatever you have to do to stay in business until the business is making enough money to support you.

There are tremendous advantages to working for yourself, but there are also risks and costs. To succeed, you must take the "risk" of putting yourself out there, maybe staking everything you have. And you must "spend" the energy to get the work and make the business happen.

Plenty of indexers have taken a more gradual approach to freelancing, working part- or even full-time while they developed their expertise and their clientele on the side. I chose, or rather I had to start as fast as I could. I needed the money and I had no real alternative to investing my time in the one thing I could see worth doing: indexing.

There are sudden and gradual approaches to just about everything. Both paths are effective, and the path you end up taking is never altogether of your own making. It is invariably a combination of disposition (or style) and fortune (or fate). I have wanted to share some of the elements that made a fast start possible for me.

Good luck!

(Reprinted from Key Words *1/4, Jan/Feb 93, page 4.)*

How to Market Your Services

By Jessica Milstead

(Jessica describes the way she makes sure that potential contacts know that she's around and what she can do for them. Hers is a specialized business with a particular clientele, but her ideas are adaptable by any freelance indexer: she networks, she writes, and she speaks.)

A number of my friends in ASI have asked me: "Jessica, just what is it you do?"

I would like to start by answering that question. I am a full-time freelance consultant. Most of my business is development of thesauri and indexes for database publishers, index publishers, and corporate clients. My clients have included firms like the H.W. Wilson Company, but I have also developed in-house databases for corporate and government clients. In other words, the bulk of my business is somehow involved with terminology and development for big indexing projects.

I purposely keep my business small. I work with other freelancers and independent contractors, but if I wanted to go back to being a manager I would opt for the security of a salary and benefits. My payoff for the insecurity of working freelance is the independence and the ability to work hands-on rather than through others.

I do make a few indexes each year, usually big ones that I design and contract out. I do get calls for indexes of the kinds I would rather not do. This work is referred to other ASI members, mostly using my personal contacts (with people who network with me) and the Register.

How did I get where I am? My background is different from that of most indexers. After receiving my master's and doctorate in Library Science from Columbia University, I taught in library schools for 10 years. I did research, and developed a professional reputation. Then I went into industry, and for a number of years with two different companies developed and edited large indexes and databases, including a now-defunct index to *The Washington Post*, for Research Publications, Inc. I also was editorial director of NewsBank, Inc., which selects articles from newspapers around the country, puts the articles on fiche, and then produces what was then a paper index to the articles. They are now available on CD-ROM. From NewsBank I went independent.

So how do I get business? Actually, what I do is talk, in public and one-on-one, and write. I would like to share with you a secret about myself. Anyone who has heard me speak can easily tell that I am perfectly happy to talk in front of a group of people. Not only does it not bother me in the slightest, I actually enjoy the experience. I have heard that Johnny Carson is the same way—no surprise at all there. But put either of us at a cocktail party among strangers— well, forget it. So I don't enjoy going out to hustle business.

I intentionally network and keep networking all the time with my friends and professional colleagues. This is adequate because I keep my business small. If I were trying to build a sizable firm I would have to market on a much more intensive scale. I attend many meetings. Every year at tax time I am astonished at the cost of my memberships and meeting attendance. But that is how I get business.

The friends and professional colleagues I see at these meetings pass along referrals.

It is important to note that my professional activities are not limited to thesaurus development. My activity in ASI is an example. I don't do much indexing business, but it's a related area. Other referrals come from people in corporate information settings or academic research. Someone knows someone who knows someone else. Second- and third-hand referrals bring in business.

For example, a couple of years ago I did a small job on the West Coast that, while well within my capabilities, was only marginally related to my current specialty. It came to me because someone called someone else who happened to know that I was on the West Coast from time to time. So this job, for which the client could not have justified the cost of bringing me from the East, came my way because my friends and acquaintances knew what I was doing.

My business has its ups and downs—whose doesn't? Before the official recession of the past couple of years, I had my own recession, when in three months I billed exactly 14 hours. A big contract that was supposed to occupy me almost full-time for somewhere between nine months and three years vanished on two weeks' notice.

What did I do? I looked around and *thought* about what I might do that would contribute to improving business in the future—and that brings me to writing.

One of the things that had been disturbing me as I developed thesauri was that all of my clients wanted to find out about software packages. I kept looking, but there was no information about software packages for thesaurus management. I decided that while business was slow, I would become the source of that information.

I went out and found everything I could about thesaurus management software packages that are available in the United States today and set out to write an article. Before I knew it, the one article had turned into three. Those articles were published in 1990 and 1991, and I still get calls based on them.

Thus, the way I market my services today is by:

- Figuring out which meetings the people I want to see will attend, then going to those same meetings and being very visible.
- Writing occasionally for the journals that the people I want to reach read.

These activities are adequate to bring in the business I need today, but what about five years from now? The information business is changing, and both indexing and thesaurus development are going to require different skills in the near future. Practically all indexers are computer-literate today; we wouldn't give up the software that automates all sorts of clerical activities. My work in thesaurus development is the same way. But there are packages on the market today that go beyond this to contribute the intellectual work of indexing, and some of them are having an impact.

Therefore, part of my marketing is future-directed. If you read my article in the November-December 1992 *Key Words* you can guess what that future-directed marketing involves. I make it a point to be aware of the capabilities of new systems and research and to be known to be aware. As a result, I am working with clients today who are exploring the potential of knowledge bases and expert systems.

I expect still to be building thesauri five years from now, but those thesauri will be designed more for machine than human application. Being part of the Information Society requires us to look to the future and plan for changes in our work. Then we can develop the skills required before our old skills become obsolete.

My approach to marketing can be taken by anyone, even though details will differ. I look for ways to make sure that potential contacts know I'm around and what I can do for them. I keep up to date, and I try to look for opportunities in unexpected places.

(Reprinted from Key Words 1/6, May/Jun 93.)

Getting Started on Your Own

By Hazel Blumberg-McKee

(In this offering, Hazel shares with us a letter of advice she wrote recently to a friend who is launching an indexing career and looking for ideas on how to market her services. In it, Hazel covers nearly all the bases of how to promote yourself as an indexer.)

Dear Linda:

I was so excited to hear that you'd left your job and become a full-time freelancer! Congratulations! I don't know how you did it all those years: putting in 40-plus hour workweeks at your publishing house job while spending evenings and weekends on freelance editing, proofreading, and indexing. I think you'll be a lot happier working for yourself. I realize that much of the freelancing you've been doing has come from your (now ex-) employer, that you're worried about how to find additional clients, and that you're none too comfortable with getting out there and promoting yourself. Despite being a full-time freelancer for the past six years, publicity is still pretty scary for me, too. Still, as a freelancer, you're now chief cook and bottle washer. If you don't want to hire PR people (and I wouldn't recommend it—too darned expensive), you'll have to do it yourself. You asked for some suggestions, so here they are:

1. Books to Read

There are a number of books I've found to be very helpful. Not all of them relate to indexing specifically (and I know that's what you'd like to be doing more of), but all of them will give you good tips on self-employment and publicity. Granted, I bought some of these books years ago, so there may be far newer editions. Check them out.

- a. Eberts, Marjorie and Margaret Gisler. *Careers for Bookworms and Other Literary Types*. Lincolnwood, Ill.: VGM Career Horizons, 1990.
- b. Edwards, Paul and Sarah. *Working from Home*. Los Angeles: Jeremy P. Tarcher, Inc., 1985.
- c. Faux, Marian. *Successful Free-Lancing*. New York: St. Martin's Press, 1982.
- d. Hanson, Nancy Edmonds. *How You Can Make $20,000 a Year Writing (No Matter Where You Live)*. Cincinnati: Writer's Digest Books, 1983.
- e. Yudkin, Marcia. *Freelance Writing for Magazines and Newspapers*. New York: Harper & Row, 1988.

2. The American Society of Indexers (ASI)

Whatever you do, join ASI! It is, after all, the only organization in the country concerned solely with indexing. There's probably a chapter in your area; if there isn't, why not put an announcement in your local paper that you'd like to get together with other indexers? There are probably a number of other indexers out there who long for contact with others. Check the ASI Membership Directory's geographic index for indexers in your area, and call the ASI Office in Seattle, (206) 241-9196, about starting up a chapter. Be sure to put an ad in the ASI *Indexer Locator*, stressing your special areas of expertise. I've gotten lots of clients that way: one publisher called me because I was the only person listed who knew Dutch, and that was a very important qualification for the indexing job at issue.

3. Indexing for Free

I realize that although you've done some indexing at your former job, you feel you don't have extensive indexing experience. Have you considered the possibility of doing an index for free? For example, in the reference section of your library, there may well be a book that's used a lot, but that (believe it or not!) doesn't have an index. Talk to the reference librarians and see if there is such a book; if there's one that a lot of people use, the librarians would probably be very grateful to you if you prepared an index to it. You'll have helped them, and you'll have earned credibility for yourself.

4. Networking

Make sure that you tell absolutely everybody that you've now become a full-time freelancer! And I do mean everybody. You never know what can happen: perhaps someone you tell has a friend who's a professor at a local college who's recently written a book, had it accepted for publication, but is at wits' end trying to figure out how to get it indexed. Is there a writers' group, an editors' group, an organization devoted to self-employed people, a businesswomen's organization, a group concerned with an interest or hobby of yours in your area? Get out there and join it! Go to meetings armed with your business cards (see suggestion #5). Who knows what business you may get as a result? And even if you don't, you'll have met people with similar concerns. It's good to have a support group out there. And you'll help to ward off the feeling of isolation that can so often descend on those of us who work all day at home alone.

5. Business Cards

While you're telling absolutely everybody that you've embarked on a whole new way of life, be sure to press your business card into their hands. It's much more professional than just scribbling your name and number on a piece of scrap paper, and it's less likely to get lost. Lots of photocopying shops make up business cards very inexpensively. Don't worry about a name or a logo for your business just yet; all that will come in time. Make sure your card contains your name, address, phone number, and what exactly it is that you do. You'll look like a pro, and you won't have blown your entire budget in doing so.

6. Local Institutions

Remember that hypothetical professor with the hypothetical book that needs an index? There may be lots of not-so-hypothetical folks around who need an index prepared and who don't know where to turn. Go around to local colleges, universities, law schools, community colleges, vocational-technical schools, libraries, you name it, and put your business cards up on bulletin boards there. If you feel you've got a definite area of expertise, wander into that particular department and chat with the departmental secretary. I'll bet he or she will know someone who needs an indexer's help. Talk to reference librarians at all these places and ask for their advice. They may be able to suggest schools, publishers, and businesses you'd never even thought of that could use your services. I've discovered that there are many small publishers out there that need indexing help; you may never have heard of them, but a well-informed librarian may. There are also many businesses that need indexes to reports, product catalogs, computer manuals, personnel manuals, in-house training materials, and so forth.

7. The Media

Most people (despite all of the American Society of Indexers' efforts) have never heard of indexing as a career. Honest! They think that elves come in the night and prepare indexes, or that computers generate indexes automatically, or some such balderdash. Call up your local newspaper's business department and briefly tell the business writer what you do for a living. I'll bet he or she will be intrigued. Offer to send a more detailed written description of your job. There's a good chance that a reporter will find you newsworthy enough to include in an article about unusual businesses. ASI has a Press Kit you can offer to send along, too, that will have ideas and background material for articles. Don't worry about being pushy; if the reporter's not interested, he or she will tell you. And don't overlook smaller, "freebie" newspapers in your area; they may be even more receptive.

8. *Writer's Market*

Writer's Market is a terrific sourcebook that comes out every year; it's published by Writer's Digest Books in Cincinnati. Either buy a copy (it costs about $25.00), or take a look at it at your local library. *Writer's Market* lists (among many other things) lots of book publishers in this country and abroad, their addresses and phone numbers, an editor's name (you might want to call the company to confirm that is indeed the current editor's name), what sorts of books the publisher produces, how many titles the publisher averages each year, and the like. One of the book's indexes lists publishers' subject areas. Look up your area of interest or expertise, and you'll no doubt find publishers that produce books on it. I use this reference book a lot.

Every few months, I'll write to a few publishers whose books intrigue me, explaining what I do, what my experience and areas of expertise are, and how I can help them. I then say that I'll call them "during the week of _____" (about two weeks away) to find out if they can use my indexing services. Sometimes they'll call me before the two weeks are up to say they're interested or not. Usually, I'll have to call them. Sometimes I prepare a "script" for myself, so that I won't get all flustered; honestly, it gets easier with time. I've gotten quite a number of clients this way—and it saves me from the scariness of the completely "cold call." At least the editor is alerted that you'll be calling.

Have I answered some of your questions about marketing yourself? If I think of anything else, I'll drop you another note; if you have questions, please write back. More likely than not, you'll have discovered a way to promote yourself that's never occurred to me at all, so please let me in on it! Good luck; I know you'll do just fine.

Your friend,
Hazel

(Adapted from ASI Newsletter, *Number 107, Nov/Dec 1991, page 9.)*

Keeping Editors Happy

By Sylvia Coates

(Do you know your editors' preferences? Here are some suggestions that will help you keep those hard-earned clients. Sylvia interviewed several editors to learn about their problems with indexes and indexers. Here she presents the results of her research: How to Avoid Becoming Your Clients' Pet Peeve.)

Indexing is a profession which seems to have an enormous turnover. Is this because many beginning indexers are simply not able to secure enough work? Assuming that the same level of competency exists, why is one indexer more successful in securing work than another?

In order to answer this question I decided to take an informal survey of several editors. Who better, I thought, to tell us why a particular indexer will receive work from them over others? In posing my inquires to these editors, I asked them to assume that the indexers in question all had the same level of competency. The majority were very eager to express themselves regarding this issue, and their answers were quite revealing.

Speak to Me!

Communication between an editor and the indexer is a crucial requirement in the working relationship. Many spoke at length regarding maintaining contact during the project. One editor specifically looks for a high level of involvement in the project. All stated that they appreciate the indexer flagging problems in advance rather than waiting till the last minute.

Late?! What Do You Mean, Late?

A particular pet peeve is to be informed at the last minute that the index will be late. Several said that having the index come in a few days late was generally not a problem but *only* if arranged in advance. In others words, don't call the morning of the due date and expect the editor to be delighted with your announcement. And while many projects may have some time flexibility there will be others which have absolutely no slip time available. One editor shared with me her worst experience with a late index: the indexer had failed to make a back-up disk of the work in progress. A hard drive failure, resulting in losing the entire project, caused the index to be turned in over two weeks late.

Causing the editor to miss a typesetting schedule can be fatal to your relationship. It shows a lack of professionalism that can cost you any future work.

Can You Follow Instructions?

Good communication also includes listening to the editor's needs. Several editors mentioned that they do not appreciate making specific indexing requests only to have them ignored. Also, once they have worked with an indexer, editors found it annoying to have to repeat their standard format requirements. They expect the indexer to have retained this information. [*Our Feb/Mar '93 issue contains, on page 18, an excellent index format checklist designed by Elsie Lynn. Another very thorough check-off list forms Appendix A, Index Specifications Worksheet, of Nancy Mulvany's text,* Indexing Books. *Use either of these checklists to ask all the pertinent questions up front, and then keep it in your permanent file for that client.* —Ed.]

The surveyed editors were united regarding the importance of following instructions. Another editor related her latest indexing nightmare: an indexer was asked to update an index to accommodate several articles which were either being added to or deleted from an already existing collection. The indexer was given a database containing the existing index and asked to add in the new entries. Instead, the indexer began to reconstruct the existing document and turned in an index which contained entries to text which didn't exist and leaving out much of the new text. The entire job had to be redone.

One can speculate that perhaps the original index was inadequate and required a new construction. Or perhaps the original index was well done and the indexer simply made a mess of what should have been a simple revision. But even without knowing such details of this nightmare it is clear that the indexer not only failed to follow the given instructions but did not maintain communication with the editor.

How About the Content?

Another editor shared with me a content issue. Her press no longer uses an indexer who began turning in long indexes which contained entries for inappropriate, superficial mentions of topics. The editors at this press didn't like having to edit out the superficial entries. They all felt that the indexer should be sending indexes with more complete editing. Eventually, even though this indexer had been used by this press for a number of years, they quit calling her. Again, causing the editor extra work is a sure way to end the business relationship.

Several editors mentioned the importance of the author's input. The author reviews the index, and, while some may be rather indifferent, there will be some who have either very positive or negative responses. Naturally, editors are always pleased to deal with happy authors, but an unhappy author is another matter. One editor said that she felt uncomfortable having to defend an indexer's work, even when she considered the index to be acceptable. Another editor feels a strong offense is the best defense. She makes it a point to hand the indexer a list of entries which the author wants included. Unfortunately, this issue is one over which an indexer may have very little control. Many authors do not have the training to accurately access an index and indexers are at the mercy of what is often an unfair judgment.

What authors *are* able to accurately judge is the subject expertise apparent—or lacking—in the index. The editor who has to explain to the author why crucial entries are missing is going to be upset with the indexer. Subject expertise is something which editors feel justified in considering when hiring, since familiarity with the topic can have a serious impact on the usability of the index. Editors were very verbal in their reactions to indexers who pretend to be knowledgeable on a subject and then produce incomplete indexes.

Clean Up Your Act!

Presentation is another issue with editors. The main message from all of the editors was: don't make extra work for them. Editors, without exception, want a final product that is as clean as possible. Though they do expect to have to review the index, there is generally a high level of competency expected from professional indexers. Expectations include consistency in the indexing, a professional appearance, and a level of indexing which is appropriate to the text.

Two editors specifically mentioned receiving hard copies on which the indexer had failed to separate the pages and generally prepare the copy for the editor. One editor, while admitting that it might be petty, stated that she resented indexers who sent in such copies. The editor said that she felt that the indexer was imposing upon her by requiring that she complete the job of decollating the printout. There were also complaints about hard-to-read typeprint. Good, dark ribbons are appreciated by editors. When the index is not presented in a professional manner, the editor receives the message that his or her time is not valued by the indexer.

Locations and Relations

Only one editor mentioned that the indexer's location made a difference. While admitting that geography, due to modems and express services, shouldn't be an issue, he simply felt more comfortable hiring local indexers. However, location does not generally seem to be a problem with most editors.

A good personal relationship with the editor is also helpful in securing additional work. An indexer's behavior toward an editor can determine whether the relationship runs smoothly or becomes strained. While this may not affect the quality of your work it may have a direct impact on repeat work. Again, this may place an unfair burden on an indexer who has to deal with unreasonable demands or an editor's abrasive manner. In that case, an indexer has to decide if it is worth maintaining the working relationship.

Helpful Résumés

The managing editor of a prestigious academic press made some interesting comments regarding marketing by indexers. She currently has a large pile of indexer résumés on her desk but not one includes a sample index. This editor said that a résumé is more likely to receive her attention when it is accompanied with a sample of the indexer's work. A résumé alone is seldom enough for an editor to make an accurate assessment of the indexer's capabilities. It is also helpful if an indexer lists references, including phone numbers, rather than simply stating that references can be provided if requested.

To sum up, editors expect a high level of professionalism from freelance indexers. They want good communication, a high-quality final product, and timely delivery. Editors want a minimum of trouble, work, and expense. Especially, keeping costs down is appreciated. If an indexer causes the press extra expense due to lateness, incomplete work, or other mistakes, the editor is not likely to rehire that individual.

In other words, make life easy for an editor and you are likely to make the top of the hiring list.

(Reprinted from Key Words *1/6, May/Jun 93, page 8.)*

Marketing Your Indexing Services:

An Adaptation of a Workshop Presented by Anne Leach at the 1996 ASI Annual Meeting in Denver

Marketing: Getting Used to the Idea

What is marketing?

According to Paul and Sarah Edwards, it is "selling or offering for sale" a product or service: "The activities involved in making sure the people who need what you have to offer know about you and are motivated to choose to work with you" (from *Making it On Your Own*, Paul and Sarah Edwards, from Tarcher Putnam, 199, p. 36).

Why does every freelancer, even a long-established one, need to market herself?

For beginning indexers, the first and best reason to find clients is to keep on paying the bills. That it's not easy to break in to a new profession is attested to by the fact of ASI's new-member attrition. We lose about a third of all our new members after the first year.

For established indexers, a reason to keep finding new clients is to replace strayed ones. Publishing houses go in and out of business or are bought up by bigger ones. Your editor is promoted, laid off, or goes freelance, and her replacement brings his own Rolodex of trusted indexers. Or publishing houses change policies and decide to encourage authors to do their own indexes, or to require their technical writers to index their own material, or to use "indexing software" that creates "indexes" automatically. Or a new indexer with a good sales pitch may have gotten to your editor. Or you may have screwed up on a job—and it only takes once. Or while you're on vacation, temporarily disabled, or, ah, overbooked, a new indexer squirms her nose under your client's tent.

Another reason you may want to find new clients is to expand into new subject areas. How boring the same old topics are! How much more interesting and/or lucrative might another subject area be?

So, we *have* to market ourselves.

But why do we view selling as a distasteful chore?

Firstly, because of its negative flavor. The stereotypical view of a salesperson is full of unflattering connotations: pushy, hustling, cocky, over-confident, brash, proselytizing, over-persuasive, interruptive, obnoxious, annoying. Or, in the case of unwilling salespeople, we think "poor guy, he must be really down and out to be doing this." Note that these negatives involve an image of someone pressuring or imposing upon someone else who is resistant, unwilling, or uncomfortable.

39

Secondly, we indexers in general are not temperamentally inclined toward the outgoing gregariousness that we usually associate with successful salespeople. (If we'd loved selling we'd have gone into sales!) We are book lovers. We are inclined to be overly orderly. We enjoy the autonomy of our work. We like being the sole decision-makers about the index. We are detail-oriented. We do not enjoy risk-taking, self-assertion, or rejection. We aren't natural-born salespeople. We like working alone; we are exacting, technical, and shy.

But we are also intelligent, dedicated, trained, and determined to do well that which we undertake. We can be persuasive when we care about an issue and have boned up on it. We are curious and creative.

And as is true in the bacterial world, necessity is the mother of mutation, so it can be with shy, unsocial indexers.

How can we learn to market ourselves successfully, despite our distaste for the task?

Firstly, by concentrating on the adaptable facets of our "Indexer Personality." Those are:

- Intelligence
- Attention to detail
- Dedication
- Non-threatening personas
- Consistency
- Persistence
- Analytical and time management skills
- A wordsmith's communication skills

All these inherited traits and learned skills are necessary to becoming a good salesperson, and indexers tend to have them already.

Secondly, we can "mutate." We usually have (or can *pretend* we have) traits upon which we can build the other skills necessary to successful marketing. Those are:

- The ability to build relationships
- A willingness to take risks
- A desire to succeed beyond our technical competence as good indexers
- The ability to survive rejection
- Creativity and curiosity about the world in general and our chosen areas of specialization
- The ability to persuade people that good indexes matter and that we can create them

And finally, we can learn to market ourselves successfully by overcoming our negative reaction to the idea of sales. We do this by concentrating on some of the positives of the process of offering for sale a product or service:

- Our product (a good index) is useful to book buyers and book manufacturers
- Really good indexes are rarer than you might think
- The service (on-time, properly formatted, already-perfect indexes) is valuable to editors
  - As we've seen, indexers do come and go, so your offer of services may be the answer to an editor's prayer

We can become eager, even excited, about finding ways to let potential clients know how we can help them, serve them, improve their working lives a little, make the publishing process easier for them, and their books better.

OK. Now that we've done a little attitude adjustment, what are the techniques of marketing that we will now implement?

The Five Keys to Successful Marketing

Key # 1: Build a Relationship.

Marketing your services is a matter of initiating and building relationships with editors—or other folks such as writers or project coordinators who hire indexers—and letting them see that they want good indexes *and* a good indexer.

Keep in mind when you initiate contact that you have a valuable service to sell, and that your services are in demand. Speak up and speak out—you can be confident that what you're offering, they need.

Begin from the point of view that you both know that good indexes help sell books. Assume high competence on the editor's part. Assume he or she is friendly and nice.

Say something like, "My name is Anne Leach, and I'm a freelance indexer specializing in (whatever) and I would appreciate a chance to work for you on an upcoming project." Or, "I'm Anne Leach, a freelance indexer, and I would be grateful if you would consider me when assigning projects for indexing."

Wait for a response. Then analyze what you're hearing. Listen carefully. Does the editor sound hurried, harried and overworked? Talk briefly about your trouble-free formats and electronic files that convert effortlessly. Is the editor laid back and loquacious? Talk about minutiae of index style and usability. Is the editor a pontificator or pronouncer? Ask questions, such as on index style preferences, and offer agreement and compliments to the house's publications. Can't decide yet where the editor is coming from? Ask questions and go ahead slowly.

Be flexible. Adapt your response to what you're hearing.
Be polite and nice.
Be friendly and professional.

Remember that editors are human, too. Talking to a person on the phone can be as personal as a face-to-face meeting, and they're relating to you, too. They'll be gentle in their treatment of you (most are female, if that means anything) and will try to be

42

accommodating and considerate of your feelings. Their response will rarely be outright rejection or rudeness. You're unlikely to encounter an ogre. (But if you do, just thank her for her time and write her off as a jerk!)

Just for fun, here is a silly scenario that will give you a glimpse into how such a telephone conversation could play itself out:

[In this scenario, Marty Indexer, who has degrees in astronomy and hotel management, hopes to gain a new client. This is his/her first call to this editor, who does hire freelancers. The editor is Spock Skywalker, managing editor of Outer Galaxies Press, publishers of dozens of books per year on interplanetary travel, UFOs, and earth visits by aliens.]

Indexer: Good morning, Mr. Skywalker. My name is Marty Indexer and I am a professional indexer specializing in intergalactic hospitality issues. I understand that Outer Galaxies Press does hire freelancers, and I would appreciate your giving me an opportunity to show you the high quality of my work.

Skywalker: We already have a number of freelancers we use, but now and then we do get in a bind and need someone in an emergency. I'll be glad to keep your name in file.

Indexer: That's great. May I send you my résumé and references as well?

Skywalker: OK. Here is the mailing address: 123 Stargazer Way ...

Indexer: Great. I'll confirm the spelling of your name and your title, if I may: S-P-O-C-K S-K-Y-W-A-L-K-E-R, and you're Managing Editor, correct?

Skywalker: That's right.

Indexer: OK. Along with the résumé and references, I'd like to send you a sample of my work that will demonstrate my skills of precision of language, elegance of phrasing, and mastery of the terminology of the field of alienology, a rapidly growing area to which your press is contributing so significantly. I do extensive reading in these areas and am familiar with most of Outer Galaxy's titles. In addition, of course, I consult the thesauri issued by the Time Travelers Association and the Science Fiction Writers Association, invaluable aids to the synonymy most helpful to those informed readers who purchase your books.

Skywalker: Really. I guess I, ah, wasn't aware there was such a thing. Interesting. Hmm. Good. OK, send me the sample.

Indexer: And if I may, I'll call you in about 10 days after you've had a chance to review my résumé and work, to answer any questions that may occur to you.

Skywalker: OK. Ah, well, as a matter of fact, we have a title coming up in a week that may be needing an index, because the author was going to do the index herself, but has been a little under the weather after undergoing Venusian tattooing on her lips and cheekbones. And our other freelancers are all probably booked up. So maybe you could take on this task?

Indexer: I sure could. Thanks very much.

Key #2: Remember that your services are valuable and in demand.

Keep in mind that the product and service you offer are valuable ones to overworked editors and rarer than you might imagine.

Let's review the ways in which a good index helps sell books, to prove to ourselves how valuable our product is:

1. It's a truism in the publishing world that any serious book should have an index.
2. Reviewers check the index if it's available to them.
3. Acquisitions librarians won't buy indexless books (or only *very* reluctantly).
4. Textbook acquisition decisions are made based on index-led scans of book contents.
5. Educated readers expect to find an index and are disapproving of indexless books and their publishers.
6. For readers unfamiliar with the book's topic, a good index provides a link between their vocabulary and the jargon used by the author.
7. Bookstore browsers who are undecided on their purchase can get an overview of the book's scope, as well as information on a specific, narrow topic.
8. Readers who have finished the book and want to recheck a certain passage can find it by means of the index.
9. Editors demand trouble-free indexes because a well-edited index provided in electronic form to the publisher's exact typographical specifications can be a tremendous time-saver for editor *and* typesetter.
10. Editors appreciate the additional proofreading that indexers perform. We are in a position to catch errors and inconsistencies that others frequently miss, such as *The Brainteaser's Bible, Brainteaser's Bible, and Brainteasers' Bible.*

Key #3: Flexibility is vital.

Remember that building a client base through phone calls means you have just one chance to make a good verbal first impression. Your attitude will carry subliminal messages to your vocal chords, so put on your "can do" attitude internally as well as externally. It's quite normal that you should be nervous and to fear that your self-esteem may suffer some blows. Yet, smile you must. Individuals of good cheer tend to work well with others, and in making that verbal first impression on a person who might hire you, that's the first thing you want your whole persona to imply. "Downers are out ... I'm a can-do person!"

Editors give work, not because they feel sorry for you, but because they value your skills and your professional, upbeat, flexible, can-do attitude. Be calm, adaptable, capable, flexible ... a pro.

Here is another silly script to give you some ideas.

[*In this scene, Marty is calling the next name on the list, Kirk Shatner, executive director of the "Pluto and Beyond Society," publishers of about 30 titles a year on alienology. At this publishing house, the policy is to use in-house help or the authors to do indexes.*]

Indexer: Good morning, Mr. Shatner. My name is Marty Indexer, and I am a professional indexer specializing in alienology. I understand that although "Pluto and Beyond" indexes are usually done in-house, you would be amenable to hiring a freelancer from time to time for emergencies, and I would appreciate your giving me an opportunity to show you the high quality of my work.

Shatner: Well, ah, actually, all our regular indexers are returned kidnappees of aliens, although, yes, we do hire outsiders for those instances when one of our regulars is, ah, away.

Indexer: I understand completely. Of course you would favor first-hand experience. I'd like to make a case, though, for using a trained indexer whose linguistic and organizational skills lead to superior indexes, in which your book-buying public will be assured of finding every pertinent sentence in the work, superbly organized in the categories and terminology he or she will be expecting to find, and elegantly delineated in subheadings that make meaningful distinctions. That, of course, as you well know, is what professional indexers do superbly. It's a well-proven fact that bookstore browsers check out the index when making up their minds whether to buy. Do you have good buyer feedback on your present indexes?

Shatner: Well, ah, actually, we haven't the means to tell. Not many of our readers actually write to us, or at least not in languages that are decipherable on earth.

Indexer: I can see that's a fascinating problem for you. Do you ever encounter schedule conflicts, where your "regular" is obliged to try to complete multiple projects with the same deadline? I would be grateful for a chance to help out in such a case. My indexes, in addition to being of professional quality, are completely trouble-free for typesetters. I can provide any format you wish, whether *Chicago Manual of Style* or *Interplanetary Travelers Guide Guidelines*. I can provide indexes in any media, whether hardcopy, diskette, e-mail, or brainwave transmission. I can duplicate any special characters of any earth-based or known alien alphabet.

Shatner: It certainly does sound like you know the field. OK, what's your name again?

Indexer: I am Marty Indexer, and why don't I send you my résumé and a sample of my work for your files? The index I'd like to send you excerpts from is for a book I recently completed for an author friend who spent several years in the control of Martians concealed in completely successful disguise as RV salesmen in Texas.

Shatner: Really! Has he found a publisher yet?

Indexer: I would be very pleased to give him your name and number, if I may.

Shatner: Great. And give me your number. I may have a book coming in tomorrow that you could index for us. It's going to be an important one for us, and maybe a professional index would be a good idea. Better for sales, and all that.

Key #4: Sell to the editor's needs, not yours.

In advertising circles, there's an adage that goes like this: "Don't tell me about your grass seed. Tell me about my lawn!"

A company selling grass seed may want its advertising to discuss the seed itself— that it's weed-free and hardy and grows well in different soils, and so on. But an ad that simply pictures grass seed is not likely to be very effective. The customer is not thinking about grass seed; the customer is dreaming of a thick, lush, green lawn, and of course that is what the advertising should show.

As an indexer, you will certainly want your customers to know about your qualifications—your education, training, and experience. But to help make the sale, you should translate those qualifications into the client's wants and needs. This could include such considerations as your dedication to meeting the client's deadline, providing the index in whatever form the client needs, and producing an index that truly enhances the book through thoroughness and conciseness of subject coverage, accuracy, synonymy, cross-references, and elegance. In short, in addition to presenting your *curriculum vitae*, create a picture of yourself as a person who recognizes the needs of two clients: the person you're addressing *and* the end user, the reader of the book.

The moral of this tale is that we must put ourselves in the shoes of those to whom we want to sell our services. Pitch to *them*, not to our perceptions and ego needs.

An editor is much more interested in hearing about what you can do *for her* than in hearing about how you're going to do it.

Now for a final silly script:

[*In our final scenario, Marty is calling Joan Crawsworth, publisher of scores of salacious, kiss-and-tell, best-selling Hollywood autobiographies. She is herself a much-married and much-divorced former actress, born in 1910, who admits to being 67.*]

Marty Indexer: Hello Ms. Crawsworth. My name is Marty Indexer, and I am a professional indexer specializing in biographies, and I've read your three most recent titles with great interest. I couldn't help noticing that they were published without indexes. I read the interview Hedda Gabber did with you in *The National Inquisitor*, where you stated that the reason you publish certain books without indexes is that you wanted people to read the *book,* not just look in the index for their own name and read only those pages. I can certainly understand your frustration at the fact that some people—perhaps the very ones who would most benefit from the just criticisms found in your titles—won't take the time and trouble to read books.

Crawsworth: Tanks. Some a dem soitenly would benefit from a dose of trut'. Our books are more than gossip an' tattlin'. Our authors have serious gripes with the film industry an' how dose who make a very good livin' from it could improve th' situation.

Indexer: I agree! I was just going to make that very point! I will venture to say this much, if you'll permit me—a good index will help get your message across. It will do much more than just list names. In addition, it will collect all the scattered references to the important topics the author discusses, under appropriate terms that your readers cannot help but notice. If I may give you an example from your last title, *My Years on the Director's Couch* by LuLu Lolita, in an index for that book, I would have created eye-catching entries such as Directors comma absconding, despotic, impotent, incompetent, masochistic, psychopathological, sadistic, whimsical, and xenophobic.

Crawsworth: Hmmm. Plenty juicy all by itself.

Indexer: Exactly. That's what I am trained to do—pull together discrete references and collect them. ...

Crawsworth: Hold on!!! Wait!! Whadaya mean, discreet? We ain' discreet. In dis business, dat's *death*.

Indexer: I beg your pardon, I misspoke. I meant to say we pull together separate references and collect them under well-chosen terms that catch the eye of the book buyer. Like "Contracts reneged upon," or "Wardrobe mistresses, sexual tyranny of," "Animals, dangers of starring with," or "Bodybuilders, dangers of starring with." Perhaps you get the idea and agree with me that an index with such tantalizing categories would have intrigued a large number of potential book buyers, even within the industry?

Crawsworth: Yeah, I can see dat. Y'may have something d'ere.

Indexer: Yes, indeed—perhaps not as wonderful as what happened for your title by Otto Zaninger: the arrest of a famous person for throwing his drink in the author's face at Chasen's—but effective in its way.

Crawsworth: Yeah, dat was a good one and cost us a bundle to arrange. Wort' it, dho.

Indexer:	Oh. I wasn't aware ... Well, I believe a well-crafted, zingy index could be as good a sales tool as the jacket blurb for grabbing the interest of the bookstore browser. I would be grateful for an opportunity to show you what a good sales tool my indexes will be. May I send you my card and a sample index?
Crawsworth:	Yeah, sure.
Indexer:	And when do you anticipate doing another title? May I call you again in a couple of weeks to see if I might be able to help you with it?
Crawsworth:	Yeah sure. Well, I'll call *you* next week, 'cause we'll have pages for Erroll Flynnt's latest, *Down Mammary Lane*. You can do us a wowser of an index for dat one. OK. Call you next week.
Indexer:	Thanks very much, Ms. Crawsworth.

Key #5: Remember that failure is OK!

Allow yourself to fail. As detail-oriented rule-followers, we may be too self-critical. It's OK to call an editor, ask for consideration as the indexer of their next project, and be told "we already have three regulars on whom we depend for all our indexing..." because

- You'll ask him to keep you in mind just in case (send your résumé).
- Their regulars may change careers or manage to screw up.
- Their regulars may go on vacation, get sick, or get overbooked, and need a stand-in. (Now's your chance to shine.)

As Thomas Watson, founder of IBM, said, "The way to succeed is to double your failure rate."

Don't take rejection personally. Or *do* take it, and your wounded feelings, out to a consolatory dinner and then forget it.

Help defuse the sting of calls that don't bear fruit—not right away, anyhow—by using your friends for what friends are for: whining! Get together among yourselves every few weeks and swap stories. Encourage each other. Mentor each other. Go back and face the cruel world with determination and courage revived.

Remember that it's OK to fail in your efforts to connect. A "no" does not mean that you're inept, unqualified, or a failure.

You should probably expect to contact 30 to 40 editors to land one regular client. Take heart from this story:

The "No! Getter"

Perhaps you've thought about the similarities between indexing and accounting. Accountants do for the financial world what indexers do for the field of information: they review data and categorize and summarize it so that it can be found again in predictable places. Their aptitudes and personalities are a lot like those of indexers.

Once upon a time, in a large accounting firm, there was a young woman who was a highly valued junior accountant. Her work was as reliable as her personality was recessive. She was painfully shy. When the firm launched a "rainmaking" contest (a sales contest, in other words) to increase billable work, she thought she might have to resign instead of participate —until they described the rules of the "No! Getters" contest. Honors would go to the person who, through contacts with existing or new clients each week, had garnered the most "No's." Asking clients if they would be interested in hearing about the other services the firm offered wouldn't be so bad, she thought, if the rejections she imagined were inevitable weren't held against her.

The next week, in the sales meeting, she had one "No" to report. The next week, two, and the week after that, four, which won her the "No! Getter" trophy to keep on her desk for a week, plus the applause of the whole staff, and a lot of genial teasing and encouragement, which she received with pleased timidity. The following week, she had only two "nos" to report, but, also, as she blushingly admitted, she'd gotten two yeses.

Let's now review the five keys to successful marketing:

Key #1: Successful marketing is a process of building relationships.
Key #2: Your services are valuable and in demand.
Key #3: Be flexible.
Key #4: Sell to the editor's needs, not yours.
Key #5: Failure is OK!

Successful Strategies for Marketing Yourself: What are the proven, successful marketing strategies?

Decide what your market is.

This is simply a matter of selecting your specialties. The same process applies whether you're a new indexer or an established one wanting to branch into new subject areas.

A glance at a typical page from ASI's *Indexer Services* publication shows how most indexers list multiple subject areas of expertise.

How do you choose a specialty? How do you branch into a new one?

Most obviously, you choose a field related to the one in which you have a degree.

Next, take an inventory of your knowledge areas, won by experience, interest and hobbies, a former employment, or extensive reading. You're perhaps familiar with computers and have a wide acquaintance—not necessarily affectionate— with software. Maybe you've been reading philosophy or history or child psychology or journals of current affairs all your life and have gained a solid grounding in the basics, issues, and jargon. Perhaps you have been working at various jobs and consequently have a wide, disconnected, but synergistic work experience.

Choose your marketing targets from among the publishers listed in a reference like *Literary Market Place* (or for short, *LMP*) or *Writer's Market*. Here are others:

- *Publisher's Directory*
- *Directory of Small Press and Magazine Editors and Publishers*
- *Chronicle of Higher Education*
- *Writer's Digest*
- *Standard Periodical Directory*
- *Standard Rate and Data Service*
- *Ulrich's International Periodical Directory*
- *English Language Newspapers Abroad*
- *Insider's Guide to Editors, Publishers, and Literary Agents*

Naturally, there may be limitations on potential earning power if the field you select is too narrow. How many books per year are published on, say, 12th century Buddhism? So you'll want to get a sense of the field: how many books are published on the subject? The number of books published per year is part of the data on each publisher presented by *LMP*, for example. Then, ask yourself what your chances are of becoming the indexer of a goodly portion of these. If the press is a very scholarly one, do you have credentials that will impress them?

Perhaps through your contacts with other indexers, you learn of an area that interests you and that appears to produce enough new publications each year to support another indexer. You might approach a colleague and ask for advice on entering that field. If you have been a responsible, conscientious supporter of your local ASI group or chapter, you will have impressed your colleagues there. Busy indexers always encounter jobs they are too pressed to be able to take on, or that are out of their preferred areas of specialization. Make yourself, your talents, your specialties, and dedication known, and a referral may come your way.

Now you've identified a target area and publishers. Next, as a well-organized person, prepare yourself and your tools.

Polish your résumé.

You are probably familiar with the typical résumé that lists employments from the most recent backwards, in reverse chronological order.

That probably won't work for indexers.

What you should work on is a functional résumé—an ability-focused summary of skills or functional areas.

It emphasizes what you can do instead of when and where you learned to do it, and if you're a novice, it allows you to highlight indexing experience you gained on a non-paid basis. It's OK in this format to eliminate or subordinate work history that's irrelevant to the job of a freelance, contract indexer.

I've included no samples because of the wide variability in this area and because of the difficulty I anticipated in finding an indexer willing to reveal the secrets of a successful résumé. However, Matt Spence's résumé appears as an exhibit in his essay, included in this volume.

If you have indexing specialties that are widely disparate in their intellectual frameworks, and hence will need to be aimed at different target markets, think about creating a separate résumé for each, emphasizing different aspects of your background appropriate to each.

For example, if in a former life you were a systems analyst, but with your degree in literature, kept yourself sane by reading good books and literary reviews, you've got the makings of *two* perfectly good résumés that a stranger would think represented two different people (... or a schizophrenic, which may in fact be the case).

Include references—names *and* phone numbers. Don't say "references on request." That's obvious and troublesome for editors. Provide the means for instant gratification of the editor's possible wish to check you out. Just be sure to get the permission of the people you want to list, and be sure their comments will be positive.

I know. There are some big "buts" on the subject of résumés. Such as:

Q: How do I put indexing experience on my résumé if I have no previous indexing experience?

A: Get some.

Q: How?

A: With your instructor's permission use an index (presuming it was any good) you prepared for your indexing course. Then volunteer to do an index for your local library of an indexless work or unindexed collection of periodicals. Be sure you know what you're doing, and be sure the librarians are pleased with your product, and then ask for a praiseful letter. Through contacts in ASI, undertake a mentored work relationship with an experienced indexer, and do some supervised work for him or her. (That's a whole 'nother topic for discussion that we haven't space for here. Marilyn Rowland's excellent article in *Key Words* Sep/Oct 96, Vol 4/No. 5 will answer all your questions.)

Finally, I recommend that you get help with your résumé, in the form of a reference or two:

- *Résumés for Dummies* by Joyce Lain Kennedy, IDG Books Worldwide
- *Cover Letters for Dummies*, also by Kennedy, also from IDG Books
- Any of the many good books on résumé-writing in your public or local college library

Now that I've offered all this advice on résumés, I'll ask you to consider a frustrating question:

Do they really work?

Maybe not.

And certainly, they won't work if sent cold, that is, with no preliminary phone contact. One indexer sent out 300 letters with no response. I've gotten more jobs by word of mouth than by any other means, and this is true of most established indexers. Editors tell other editors, and other indexers give the names of their trusted colleagues to editors whom they themselves were too busy to help.

But I like to have my résumé updated and handy so that I can offer it to the new caller "for her files." It's more professional, I think. (And I always send a sample index along too.)

A résumé will certainly *not* work for you, indeed will work against you, if it is on cheap paper, printed on a dot matrix printer, or (God forbid) has typos, grammatical errors, or awkward diction.

A very good idea is to have your résumé (and all PR materials, such as your customized brochure) reviewed by a colleague you trust.

Another good idea is to prepare a sample index or excerpt to accompany your résumé. Naturally, if you're targeting a publisher in an esoteric field, it would be nice if the sample of your work demonstrated your familiarity with the jargon of the field, but you could also do a "generic" sample that any educated person would enjoy browsing for its own sake that demonstrated balance, consistency, and elegance.

Spruce up your professional image.

Take a critical look at the image your public gets in its first contact with you.

Letterhead, business cards, Rolodex cards, and brochures: With help from a good local printer, or with creativity, a laser printer, good quality bond paper and Avery items, clip art or a wingding for a logo, you can customize some decent paper products that present you to the public.

Answering machine message: Listen with a hypercritical ear to your answering machine's outgoing message. (You do have an answering machine, don't you?) Does your message present a professional, courteous "face" to the world? Is the message complete but concise? Polite, friendly in tone, yet businesslike? Get a friend's opinion.

Telephone image: Do the same hypercritical listening to your live telephone voice, or better, ask a friend to give you honest feedback. Is there a pleasing amount of modulation in your tones, or do you tend to speak in a depressed monotone? Is there personality and friendliness in your voice? Do you answer with a professional-sounding greeting ("Good afternoon. Mary Jones Indexing Services.") or do you just growl, "Hello." Or worse, does your small child or sullen teenager answer the phone? Do they respond, when asked to take a message for you, "Wait a minute. Hold the phone. Where's a pencil?" Do you ask the normal questions of your clients that you would ask of a friend—"How are you?" Your phone friendships will in this way develop naturally over the course of work. Soon you'll be exchanging personal news updates . . . you'll be friends.

Make time for your marketing tasks.

Carve out the time for marketing yourself. Congratulate yourself on the fact that you're an organized time-manager; set yourself the task and make yourself complete the assignment bit by bit on a methodical basis. Expect to spend several hours a week at it at first, making up to 40 contacts for each client you gain.

Prepare a plan for yourself (in writing) with dates and activities: making calls, sending résumés, doing follow-up calling, writing articles, offering and preparing presentations on indexing, and so on.

Stick to your schedule. You know your own resistances to disagreeable tasks; find ways to get yourself around the sticking points. The hardcore organization freaks among us may get more pleasure from organizing all this than from actually doing it, so live it up! Try using some scheduling software if that turns you on. Examples are (in 1997) ACT from Symantec and Microsoft Schedule+, a part of the Microsoft Office Suite of programs.

In a special notebook arranged alphabetically, or in your contact management software (a tool used by salespeople for tracking contacts), meticulously record notes of your initial and follow-up activities, so that you'll know where you are with each individual. Record especially any personal information about them that happens to arise in your conversations so you can refer appropriately to it next time, if you choose.

Tell everybody.

Contact your friends, acquaintances, relatives, local universities, former professors, libraries, and so on, and tell them of your new profession. When you know someone in the publishing industry, ask them to suggest persons you could talk to about the field of indexing and to keep you in mind should a need for an indexer arise.

Contact your local newspaper's business page editor. (This is a good idea for a chapter to undertake, too.) Discuss your indexing career as the possible focus of a feature on unusual or home-based freelance business.

Look for opportunities to spread your fame.

In the *NTPA (National Trade and Professional Associations)* directory or the *Encyclopedia of Associations,* you will find groups related to your specialty. Join those that interest you, and get involved in the chapter activities. Call the program chair of the group's local chapter and offer to speak at a meeting, on the topic of good indexes. Call the editor of their newsletter and offer an article. This strategy is more fully described in Jessica Milstead's article on pages 27-29 in this booklet.

Get online.

Join chat groups or newsgroups, monitoring these for chances to offer information on good indexing and ASI. Direct advertising is not advisable, but your signature on a helpful, fact-based response to a topic can lead to inquiries from potential clients.

Get your own Web Page

This may become even more widespread in future years. The jury is out on the question of usefulness, however. It's unknown how many publishers will shop for freelance contractors on the Web. Individual authors, I suspect, may be more inclined to find an indexer online, but an individual author may write only one book a year at most—not a good bet for regular income.

At any rate, if you're interested, consult Kari Bero's article in the Mar/April '96 issue of *Key Words*.

Advertise?

Does it work?

I don't know for sure, but I suspect not. I have been listed in *Literary Market Place* for years and have never gained a client through them. It's free, so I keep it up. ASI has maintained a barter-basis ad in *Publishers' Weekly Resource Directory* for years, too, and to my knowledge, only one inquiry has ever come to our ASI Admin office from that source. I don't believe editors have time to read it—or perhaps anything at all except what they *must* read on the job.

Write an article for Key Words.

Becoming known to your colleagues as an expert in something or other can't hurt you. Writing an article for *Key Words* will do for your expertise in a field what the discipline of good writing always does—your knowledge will be expanded, firmed, and refined by the research and thinking and verbalization required.

Mine your existing client base.

Compare your client list to your marketing To-Do chart. Are you missing any bets? Have you not heard from a potential client yet? The initial investment and contact has already been made for this person, so presumably you have a name recognition factor working for you. You can try again with a variation on your original approach, mentioning your new, recent work in the field.

If you are already getting work from several clients, you might try calling them to see if they work for companies where other imprints, or divisions of the publishing house, might have need of your services. Or, you might ask your editor/client if she happens to know if their other indexers are members of ASI. Without even *thinking* of calling these other indexers to compare notes and rates of pay, you *can* call them to introduce yourself, describe your qualifications, and ask them to consider calling you for their next overflow job. (ASI annual meetings are ideal for this kind of networking.) Keep each other in mind for referrals or subcontracting for jobs you're too busy to handle or in subject areas you don't care to tackle. Reciprocate referrals when you can. Return the favor.

Turn a move or phone number change into an opportunity.

What if, after you've spent a great deal of effort, time, and money on a marketing program, you decide to change your residence? Or the telephone company decides to change your area code?

Certainly, you'll not want all that to be lost. You can take these steps:

- For known clients (those for whom you are working now, or will be after you move), send an address change notice, either a letter or a nice card, plus several new business cards and Rolodex cards. Call too. Talk to all the editors at each publishing house, even those editors you haven't yet worked for. Why not? It's a good excuse to talk to them. You could say, "I thought perhaps Joe might have given you one of my cards, since I've been doing indexes for him for years, and he's been very pleased with my work. Anyhow, my address and phone will be changing in three weeks, and I wanted to be sure everyone who might like to call on me had correct info. May I send you my card? Is it possible you could have an overflow job sometime that you would consider sending my way?"
- It wouldn't hurt to talk to the accounting department too, or they will surely send your next check to the old address, despite the new address appearing on your invoice along with a big notice: "Please note change of address."
- For potential clients whom you've called and written to, do the same: call and write.
- And do one other very important thing. Contact your telephone company and request a number referral service on your old line. In California, one telephone company charged me only $30 for a one-year recorded referral message on my old number. However, in another year, another move, the next telephone company gave me 90 days' referral free, but for neither love nor money could I get more than the 90 days.

Keeping Your Clients

Once you've found a client, how do you keep her, and perhaps generate more clients through her? There are several questions that will come up in your initial discussions about a first job for a client, and I'll try to suggest ways to handle them that will have positive results for you.

- How should you broach the subject of money with a new client?
- What do you charge for your work?
- Should you insist on a contract?
- How many ways are there to make an editor happy?
- How do you say "No" to a job?
- How do you handle the one you wanted to decline but accepted anyhow?

How should you broach the subject of money with a new client?

We'll assume that by this time, you've been through all the preliminaries and these are the last details to be worked out before she hires you.

You can say, "My rates usually are between $X and $Y per page for the type of work you describe, but before we settle on a figure, I'd like to take a look at a sample chapter, say, the fifth chapter, and get a clearer idea of the density of the text, the layout, and so on. Then I can quote you a number with assurance that I can do a very high quality index for this book." This approach usually works.

You could ask, "Is the range I just mentioned within the ballpark for ABC Press? What do you usually pay your indexers?" If her answer is satisfactory to you, say "That will be fine." If it's higher than you were expecting or were prepared to accept, say "That will be fine" and try not to giggle.

If it's lower than you were hoping for, ask the questions below, to serve two purposes: to see if maybe the rate will be adequately remunerative after all, and to communicate subtly to the editor that maybe paying more in order to get your high-quality, trouble-free product will be worth it. (Incidentally, the following parameters are the sort of thing you will want to analyze if given a chance to index a sample chapter in advance of stating a bid for the job. I recommend you ask for a chapter from the middle of the book. First chapters are often very dense in their subject treatment, or else so broad in sketching of background, that they'll mislead you as to the text density of the bulk of the book.)

- What is the finished page size of the book? (4 x 6 goes faster than two-columned 8 x 10.)
- Are there footnotes, tables, or photo captions? (These almost always have indexable material and may take longer to analyze and characterize than plain text.)
- Are there lots of white space and subtitles? (Informative subtitles are very helpful to the indexing process.)
- What is the point size and line spacing of the typeface? (10-point at 1.1 line spacing is easier to read than 8-point at .9)
- Is the book well written for a lay audience, or will you have to read, reread, and re-reread to tease meaning out of impenetrable academese?
- Are there any unusual features of the book that will make for difficult indexing? Examples are scads of names, or Latin names of botanical specimens, or romanized names from languages other than English, or names or terms in languages, alphabets, or characters other than English. Or maybe pages of program code that you should be able to "read" in order to characterize the routines for the index. Or perhaps the work is a collection of essays by many authors, with problems of vocabulary control and theme reiteration that will complicate your task.

Based on the responses to these questions, you may be able to assess whether the job is worth it to you at the quoted rate, or if you want to try for more money. You can ask the editor if you can take the job with the understanding that you will index a typical chapter and see how it goes, and then talk money within a certain range.

What do you charge for your work?

Many indexers recommend that you do an index for free in order to have at least one under your belt and to have something to put on your résumé. I'll agree to that suggestion—but I do *not* recommend that you make a habit of giving yourself away.

Some indexers offer to do a cut-rate job in order to *get* the job. No doubt, all quality considerations being equal, this will grab an editor's attention. But you may be undercutting the professional image you're trying to build. If you respect yourself and your work as being of professional caliber, then you deserve remuneration as a professional. Editors, deep down, believe this too, despite cost-cutting impulses. If you cut your rates, your client may wonder if you're cutting your quality too, someplace or other. And . . . the fact is, you may very well be. If you're not earning a decent, living wage, your unconscious impulse may be to hurry, to skip some entries that really deserve to be created, or overlook some failures of symmetry, or forego that one last edit.

Discuss rate-setting with your colleagues. What considerations go into their rate-setting processes? These might be overheads, self-employment and income taxes, medical insurance, reserves for necessary software upgrades, etc. Get an idea what experienced indexers are charging and how they justify their charges to their clients.

Should you insist on a contract?

When both parties are happy, a contract is unnecessary. When one is unhappy, it's indispensable.

I have two kinds of clients, all of them publishers or production houses, not authors. I have never felt the need to suggest to a client that a contract be drawn up. The larger publishing houses send me a contract or "work for hire" agreement that is one page of uncomplicated language without reference to possible dissatisfaction with my product. The smaller clients, such as production houses or independent production coordinators, may send me a purchase order that simply spells out a title, a maximum number of pages, and a rate per page. Or we may be working with no paper at all—just a "handshake" deal undertaken over the telephone with someone I've never met in person.

But the subtext in my business relationships is that both parties, they and I, are experienced and responsible professionals who honor our commitments—I to provide a totally satisfactory and timely product, and they to pay for it in a timely manner at the agreed price. I have not asked them to sign a contract because, firstly, with my clients, it has not been necessary, and secondly, the only indexing contract I've ever looked at is the *ASI Recommended Indexing Agreement*, and it is, at first glance, formidable. It's necessarily full of legal language regarding obligations and unhappiness of one or both parties. A publisher or author might want to have it reviewed by a lawyer before signing it.

In other words, it's more than I've thought I needed in the way of protection.

On the other hand, I rarely work directly for an author, whose familiarity with standards in the publishing world and with proper indexing principles may be assumed to be less than that of a publishing house. If the index-ignorant author happens also to be nitpicky, argumentative, litigious, and strapped for cash, you may have a problem producing a "satisfactory" index, and/or getting paid for it. That's when you will wish you had ignored that stupid Anne Leach's comments and insisted upon a contract.

So the final point I'd like to make is that it's your judgment call whether to ask the potential client to sign an agreement that sets out the processes you'll both follow in the event of dissatisfaction. Weigh your degree of confidence in:

- The professional integrity of your potential client. Will she pay her bills? On time?
- Your ability to create a satisfactory index for the work in question
- The client's familiarity with good indexing principles, or their willingness to rely on yours
- The financial soundness of the client

If your assessment is that you'd be more comfortable with a signed agreement, then the *ASI Recommended Indexing Agreement* is an excellent place to start. It offers balanced protection for both parties, provides for stipulations for all conceivable parameters of an index so that nothing is left to chance, and is easy enough to understand. It's designed to be tailor-made for each job and is available from ASI on diskette.

How many ways are there to make an editor happy?

- Never be late!
- Follow all index format specs. To be sure you know what they all are, use a checklist such as you'll find in Nancy Mulvany's book *Indexing Books*. Cindex and Macrex are both very powerful and can do practically anything in the way of index formats.
- Deliver the index in the preferred mode: FedEx with hard copy, or a formatted file by modem or e-mail.
- Forestall any problems your client may have in translating your index file into their word processing or typesetting program. Devise suitable substitutions for diacriticals, em dashes, etc., that may not translate properly between your program and theirs.
- Provide hard copy if requested, in the format she prefers: single or double spaced? Fan-fold paper or decollated? Stapled or paper-clipped? "Continued" headings? Camera-ready?
- Provide a listing of your index entries in page number order, for perusal by the editor if she wishes. (This can be very useful in those cases of text that "walks" after they've provided you with "final" pages. Often, an editor will

prefer to make a few adjustments of your entries, using the page number order listing, and save time at the last stages.)

- Mark pages on which you find little goofs or inconsistencies. Call the client with word of these if deadlines are looming, so that corrections can be made if desired, before the expensive "blue-line" stage.
- Discuss with your client any special situations you discover in the text or its organization that present interesting indexing challenges. Suggest ways to solve the problems, and get input and concurrence from your client. This allows you to show off a little, while also demonstrating your adaptability.

How do you say "No" to a job?

Suppose an editor calls with an offer of a book you cannot take on because you're already swamped with other pressing deadlines; or you're empaneled on a jury and are about to be sequestered for weeks; or you know little about the subject except that it's more than you, as a professional, should tackle. How do you decline the job without harming the relationship with that editor?

First, remember to put the editor's needs foremost in your mind. Apologize sincerely and fluently for having to let him down. Explain why you have to. Make it clear that your professional commitment to timely provision of superior indexes and your desire to be of real service to him preclude your being able to take on this job. You would be unable to perform to your own standards and to his satisfaction in this instance. Express your fervent hope that he will call you again for a future job, because (unless you're a jury-duty junkie) this sort of difficulty rarely arises.

If it seems appropriate, you might offer to find other indexers for your client to call, and then you can consult ASI's *Indexer Services* directory. Caution your client, however, to check references and qualifications for the other individual, just as he normally would. Although membership in ASI *is* a testimonial to the indexer's concern for professional standards and standing, there is no formal testing or registration or qualification process involved in becoming an ASI member. In itself, it does not indicate competence.

How do you handle the one you wanted to decline but accepted anyhow?

Suppose you have accepted a job, reluctantly, that has a very near deadline that means you'll be pulling another all-nighter. What should be the tenor of your conversations with your difficult client?

Remember my earlier urgings about the importance of relationship-building and an upbeat attitude. Don't moan, groan and get hostile with your client if a schedule gets crunched and you're the shortstop. Besides being unprofessional, hostility and complaint will sour your relationship with that client.

Face with equanimity the main fact of life in publishing: *schedules are made to be telescoped.*

After cheerfully making clear to your client the difficulties of meeting the deadline, simply offer what you believe to be the very best possible return date, negotiate an agreement, and then meet it with an index of undiminished quality. Come through in the crunch for your client. She'll remember you gratefully.

I faced such a situation not long ago: a longtime client called with a 250-page workbook on a very short fuse. She offered a premium for the rush job. I agreed to a 24-hour turnaround and kept my promise. Then when she asked about the premium payment, I explained that a colleague's usual premium for a rush job was an additional 50 percent of the per-page total, but that I would settle for 30 percent. She insisted on paying me the 50 percent!

Asking for Referrals

When chatting with your clients, preferably after receiving his praise for the excellence of a job you've just completed, ask for referrals! Say, "By the way, I would appreciate your passing my name along to any editors you happen to encounter who are looking for a superior indexer. As you know, I do XYZ subjects, but you may not be aware that I am also a near-expert in ABC and DEF topics. My other clients in those areas are highly regarded, and I've been working for them for years."

A Final Note: Remember to Build Relationships

Your clients will come to be your friends, as well as professional colleagues, though you may never meet face to face. Let that expectation and likelihood infuse all your dealings with your clients, and you will succeed in building your indexing business.

Good luck to you, and my very best wishes for your success.

Index

Other Books on Indexing from ASI and Information Today, Inc.